1-2-3 DRAW CARTOON AIRCRAFT

A step-by-step guide

by Steve Barr

Peel Productio
Columbus, NC

D1530968

To Mrs. Verlander, my seventh grade teacher. Her wisdom, guidance and encouragement helped a little boy grow up to live an enchanted life doing something that he truly loved.

Printed in China

Library of Congress Cataloging-in-Publication Data

Barr, Steve, 1958-
1-2-3 draw cartoon aircraft : a step-by-step guide / by Steve Barr.
      p. cm. --   (1-2-3 draw)
Includes bibliographical references and index.
ISBN 0-939217-76-7 (alk. paper)
      1. Airplanes in art--Juvenile literature.   2. Cartooning--Technique--
Juvenile literature. I. Title.   II. Title: Cartoon aircraft. III. Title:
One-two-three draw cartoon aircraft.   IV. Series: Barr, Steve, 1958- . 1-2-3
draw.
   NC1764.8.A47B37 2005
   741.5--dc22

                                        2004027140

Distributed to the trade and art markets in North America by

NORTH LIGHT BOOKS,
an imprint of F&W Publications, Inc.
4700 East Galbraith Road
Cincinnati, OH 45236

(800) 289-0963

Table of Contents

Stop! Look! Listen!

Before You Begin

You will need:

1 a sharpened pencil

2 paper

3 an eraser

4 a pencil sharpener

5 colored pencils, markers, or crayons

6 a comfortable place to sit and draw

7 a good light source so you can see what you're doing!

Note: If you have trouble drawing perfect circles or straight lines by hand, it is fine to use a ruler or trace around something circular while you are using this book. Just remember...there are NO RULES in cartooning....so it's okay if your shapes and lines aren't perfect!

Let's draw cartoon aircraft!

NO RULES!

There is no right or wrong way to draw a cartoon because there are NO RULES in cartooning. If your sketches don't look just like the ones in this book when you are done, that's okay! It means you are exploring and developing a style of your own. You can use photographs of airplanes for reference and you can change anything on them that you like. Change your cartoon airplanes and make them uniquely your own. Color them any color you wish.

Sketch, doodle, and play!

The more you practice, the better you will become. Experiment with each drawing. Sketch, doodle, and play! Change anything you want as you go through this book. The more you change, the better. It's your drawing, so you can make it look however you want. If your drawing makes you smile, you are doing it right.

A few cartooning tips

1   Draw lightly at first—SKETCH, so you can erase extra lines in the final drawing.

2   Practice, practice, practice! You will get better and your cartoons will get funnier.

3   Have fun drawing cartoons!

Basic Shapes and Lines

Here are samples of the various lines and shapes you will use in this book.

Oval

Egg

Circle

Triangle

Rectangle

Kidney bean

Box (cube)

Straight line

Curved line

Square

Squiggly lines

Zigzag lines

Note: Professional cartoonists use tools to help them get their drawings just right. If you have trouble drawing a perfect circle or straight line by hand, it's okay to trace something round or to use a ruler. But, remember that cartooning has NO RULES. It is also fine if your circles and straight lines are a little shaky.

How Professional Cartoonists Work

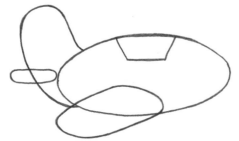

Professional cartoonists begin with an idea of what they want to draw, then try to put it on paper. Many times it doesn't end up looking exactly like the idea they had in mind. That's okay, because they know they can change and correct things as they go along.

I begin by doodling basic shapes, lightly, on a clean sheet of paper. As the drawing begins to look the way I want it to, I gently erase any extra sketch lines. I then use use a black pen to trace the final picture. Once the inked drawing is finished, I add color.

You do not need a pen to finish your final art. Practicing with pencil drawings is a great way to learn. Once your pencil sketches get really good, you might want to try experimenting with a pen to make your cartoons bolder and even better.

STEVE BARR

Blimp

Blimps can be seen drifting over football stadiums, outdoor events, and cities. They usually have advertising on their sides. Let's draw a blimp!

1 Begin by lightly sketching a large oval.

2 Look at the shapes added to one side of the oval. Using curved lines, draw these.

3 Add curved lines below the oval for a gondola.

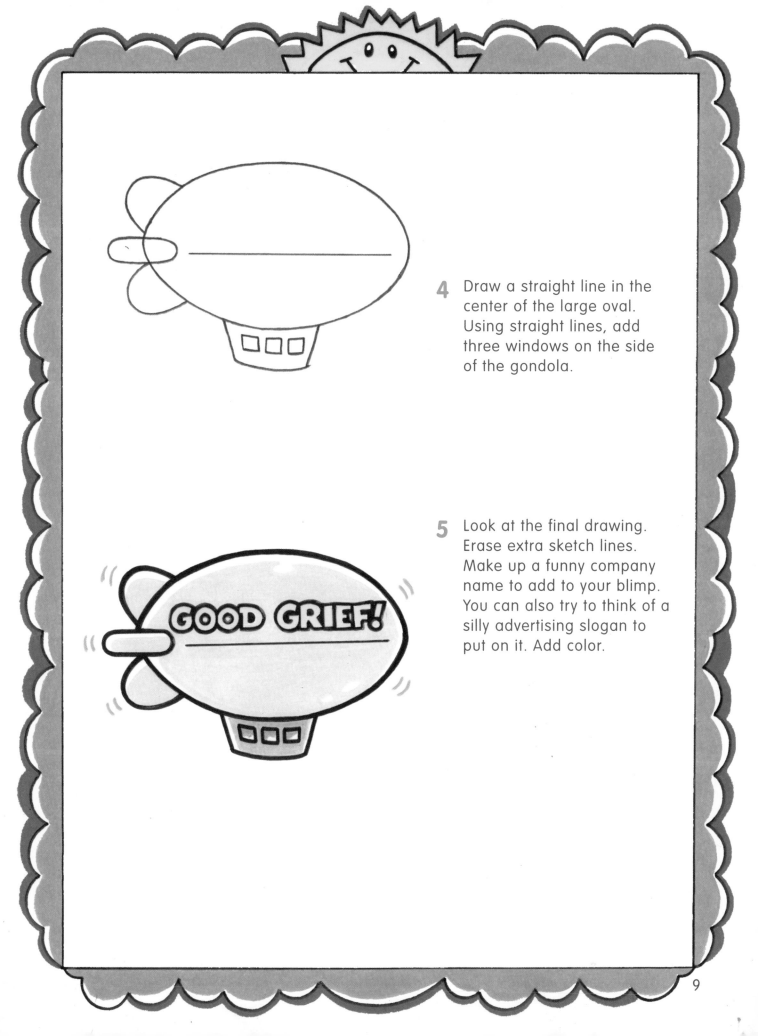

4 Draw a straight line in the center of the large oval. Using straight lines, add three windows on the side of the gondola.

5 Look at the final drawing. Erase extra sketch lines. Make up a funny company name to add to your blimp. You can also try to think of a silly advertising slogan to put on it. Add color.

GOOD GRIEF!

Hot Air Balloon

Hot air balloons look great drifting across the open sky. They have small passenger baskets on them and are usually brightly colored. Let's draw a hot air balloon.

1 Sketch a large circle.

2 Draw a small rectangle below the circle. Using straight lines, connect the two shapes.

3 Look at the rectangular shapes on the bottom that form the basket. Draw these.

4 Look at the curved lines inside the circle. Add these. Draw the oval shaped eyes. Using curved lines, draw the smiling mouth.

5 Look at the curved lines inside the top of the circle. Add these. Darken part of the eyes. Draw the lines inside the bottom of the circle.

6 Erase extra sketch lines. Darken the final lines. Add color. Draw clouds in the background.

He looks quite cheerful for being so full of hot air!

Happy Plane

You can make your cartoon aircraft come alive by giving it a face and making it a cartoon character.

1 Begin by sketching an oval.

2 Add a curved line to the oval for a tail.

3 Draw squashed ovals for wings. Add an oval for the tail wing.

4 Draw the curved windshield. Using two curved lines, begin the mouth.

5 Using small ovals, draw the eyes inside the windshield. Add more curved lines to the mouth. Draw a tongue.

6 Look at the final drawing. Erase extra lines. Darken part of each eye. Go over and darken the final lines. Add color.

Just like people, cartoon characters can change moods. Let's learn how to draw different expressions to show different emotions.

Facial Expressions

Look closely at the lines and shapes used in these drawings to show different emotions. Try drawing a few of these. Draw the outline of the plane from page 13 again and add your favorite expression.

Sad

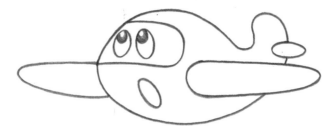

Surprised

Sick

Goofy

Mad

Really Mad!

To create more crazy expressions, try a technique used by top-notch cartoonists. Look in a mirror. Make a funny face. Look at the shapes your mouth, eyes and eyebrows make. Draw them on your plane. How do they look?

Single Prop Plane

Single prop planes have only one propeller. They are used for family recreation, sightseeing tours, and a variety of other functions. Let's draw a single prop plane!

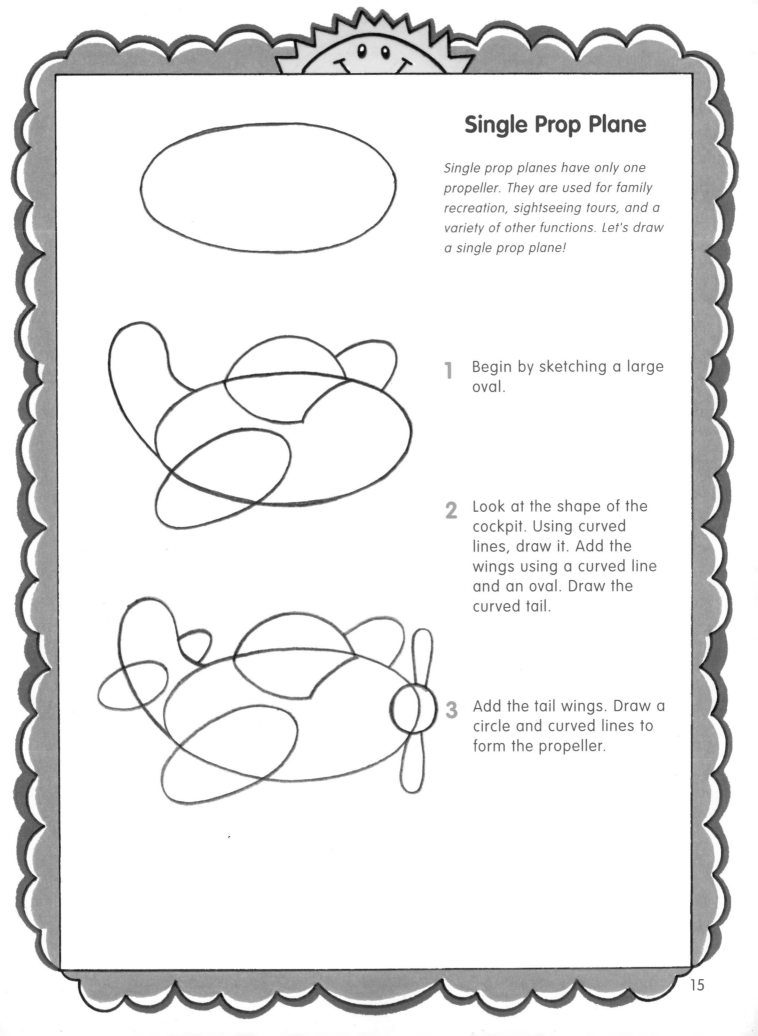

1 Begin by sketching a large oval.

2 Look at the shape of the cockpit. Using curved lines, draw it. Add the wings using a curved line and an oval. Draw the curved tail.

3 Add the tail wings. Draw a circle and curved lines to form the propeller.

4 Draw ovals inside the cockpit for eyes. Add curved body lines. Draw the smiling mouth.

5 Using curved lines, add the eyeballs. Draw curved lines for tires.

6 Look closely! Erase extra sketch lines. Darken the final lines. Color your prop plane as you wish. It's your airplane!

Note: You can make your plane look like it is soaring happily through the sky by adding dotted lines behind it. Little curved lines above and below the propeller give it the appearance of movement.

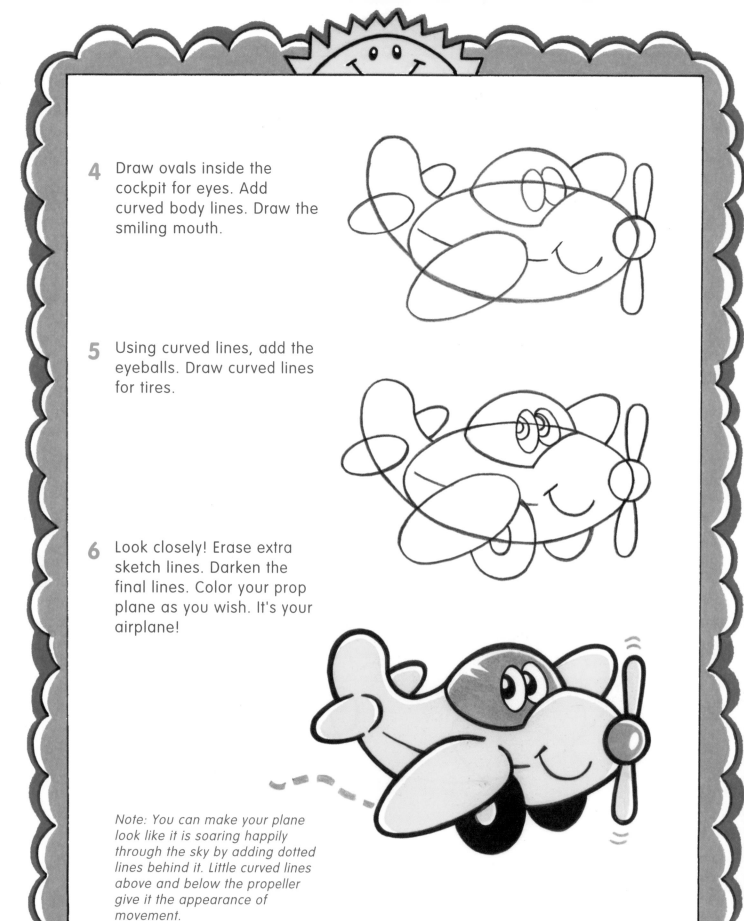

Passenger Jet

Passenger jets carry lots of people great distances in short periods of time. They have a bunch of seats, so they need to have quite a few windows on the sides. Let's draw a passenger jet.

1 Begin by lightly sketching a large oval.

2 Draw a curved line for the tail and a squashed oval for a wing.

3 Draw a small oval for the tail wing. Using curved lines, add the nose cone and engine.

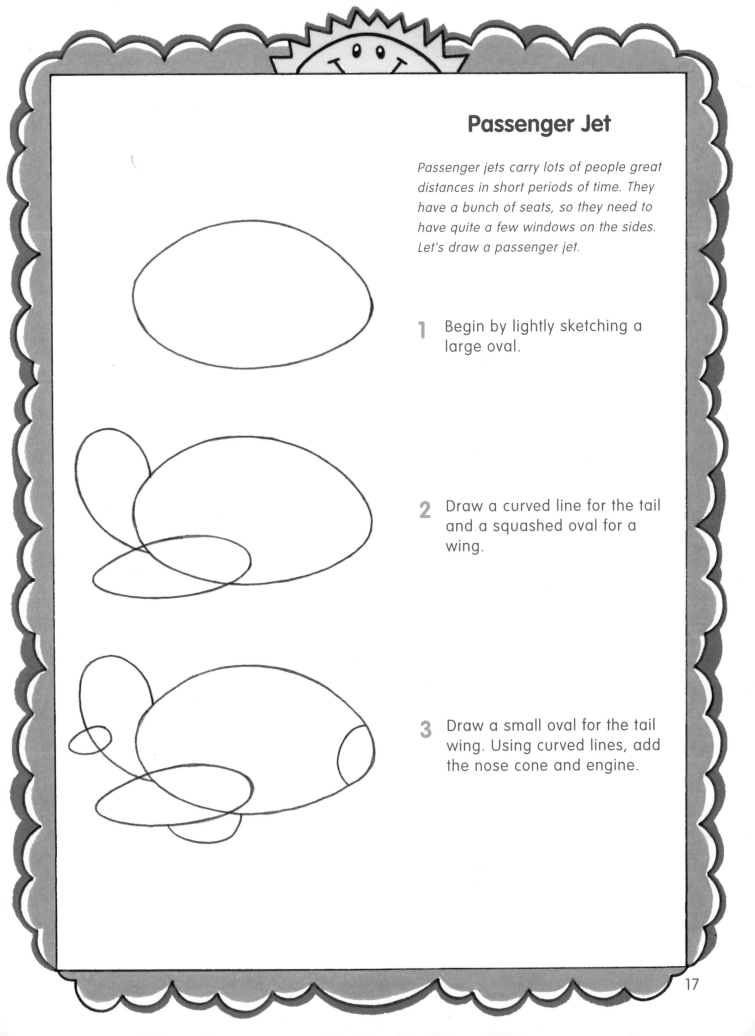

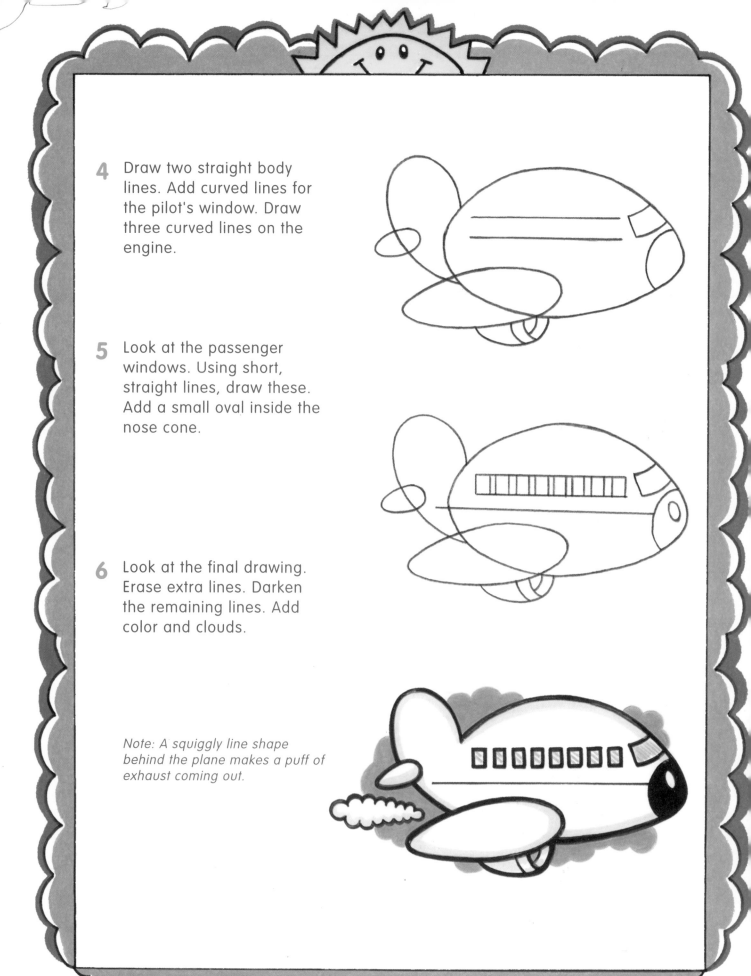

4 Draw two straight body lines. Add curved lines for the pilot's window. Draw three curved lines on the engine.

5 Look at the passenger windows. Using short, straight lines, draw these. Add a small oval inside the nose cone.

6 Look at the final drawing. Erase extra lines. Darken the remaining lines. Add color and clouds.

Note: A squiggly line shape behind the plane makes a puff of exhaust coming out.

Character Jet

Let's add an expression from a side view using the passenger jet from pages 17-18. Let's draw a happy plane.

1 Draw the outline of the passenger jet again without the passenger windows.

2 Draw an oval for an eye. Add a curved line for an eyebrow. Draw two curved lines for a mouth and pudgy cheek.

3 Darken the eyebrow. Add the eyeball. Darken part of it. Add another curved mouth line.

4 Look closely! Darken the final lines. Add windows if you like, then add color.

He certainly is a happy looking passenger jet!

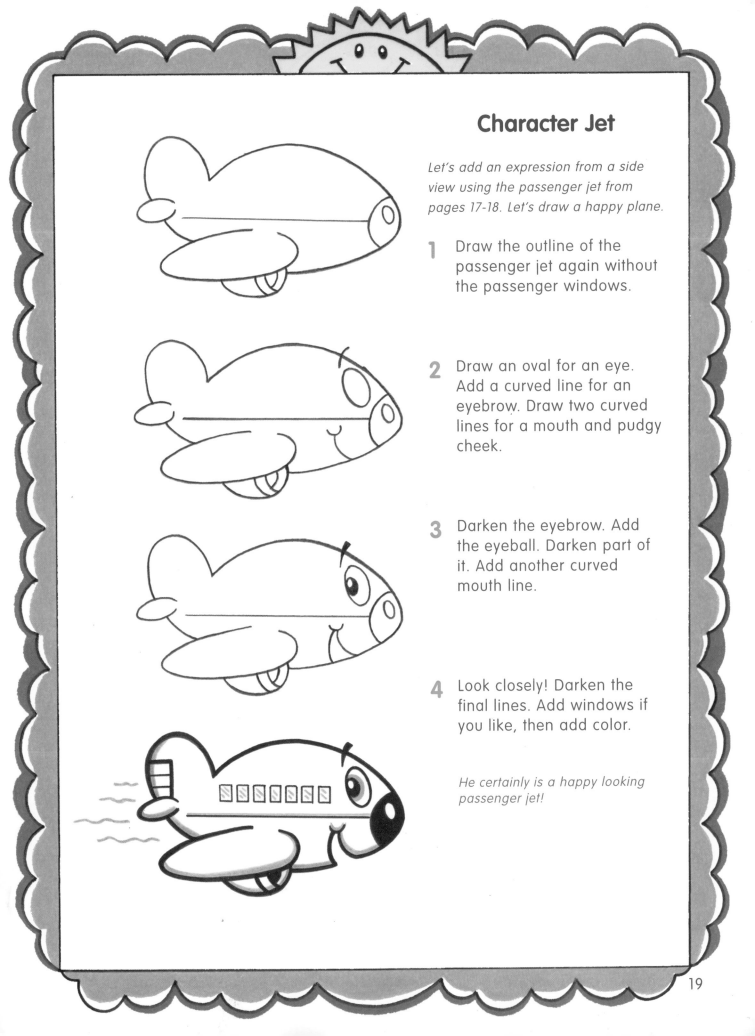

More Expressions

Look closely at the examples on this page. You can radically change your cartoon plane's character by changing its expression using simple shapes and lines. Draw some of them, or create your own cartoon airplane face.

Add eyelashes to change your plane into a girl!

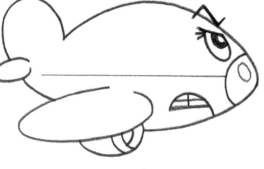

Happy

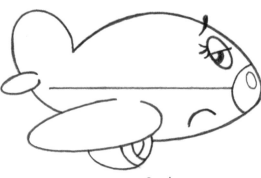

Sad

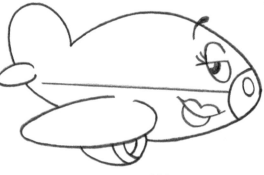

Angry

Puzzled or upset

???

Startled

Tiny Plane

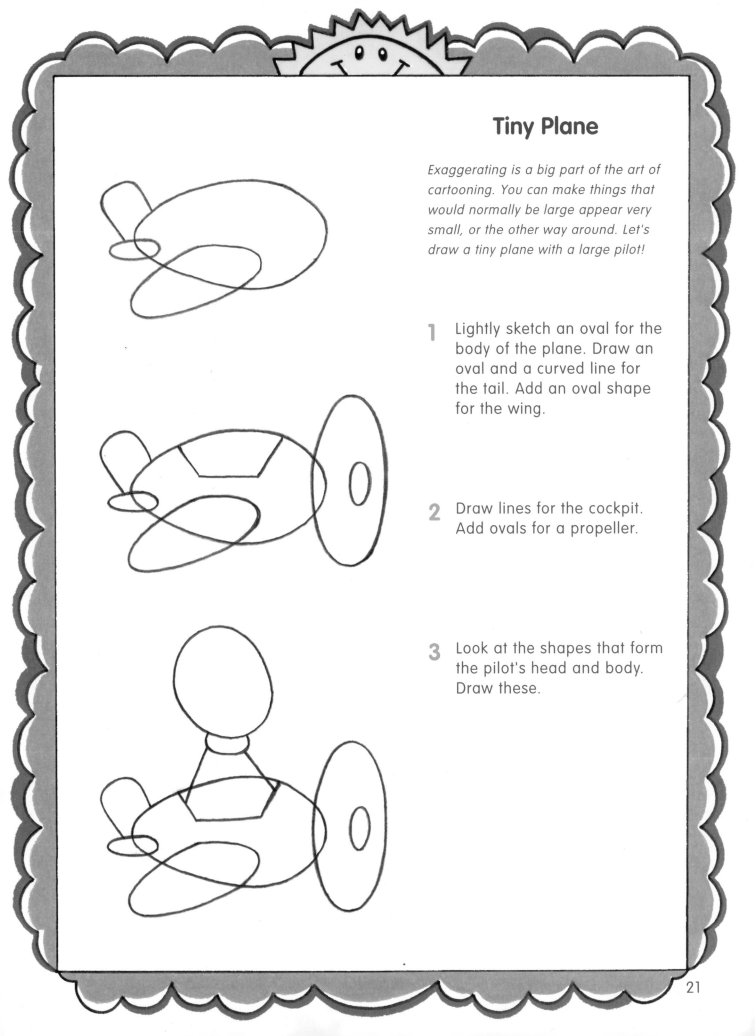

Exaggerating is a big part of the art of cartooning. You can make things that would normally be large appear very small, or the other way around. Let's draw a tiny plane with a large pilot!

1 Lightly sketch an oval for the body of the plane. Draw an oval and a curved line for the tail. Add an oval shape for the wing.

2 Draw lines for the cockpit. Add ovals for a propeller.

3 Look at the shapes that form the pilot's head and body. Draw these.

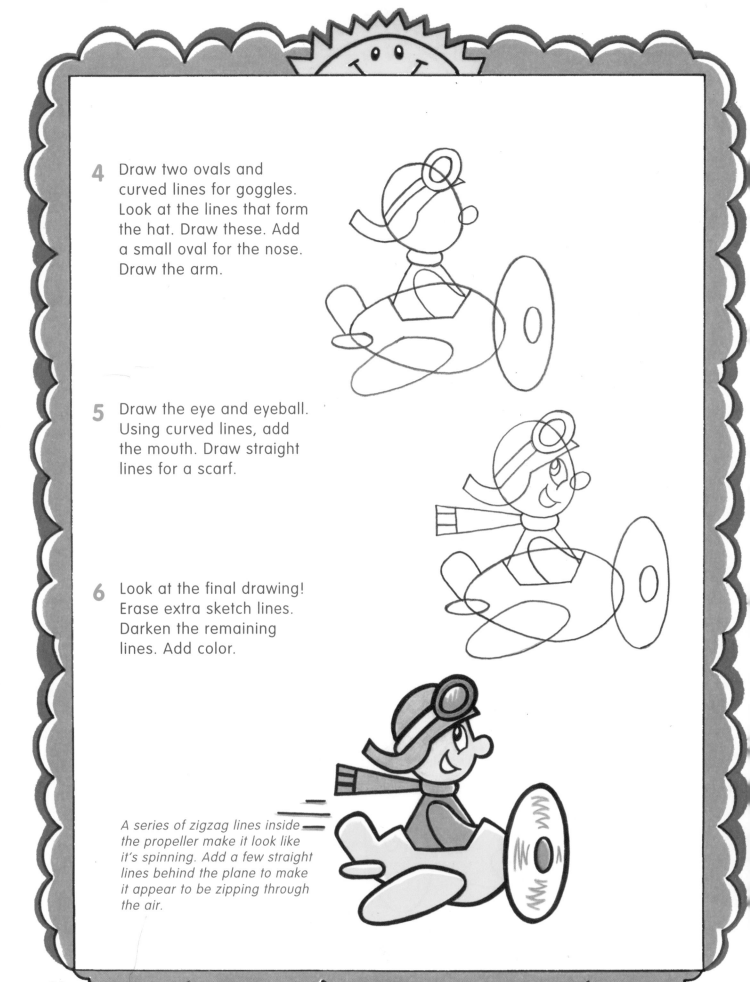

4 Draw two ovals and curved lines for goggles. Look at the lines that form the hat. Draw these. Add a small oval for the nose. Draw the arm.

5 Draw the eye and eyeball. Using curved lines, add the mouth. Draw straight lines for a scarf.

6 Look at the final drawing! Erase extra sketch lines. Darken the remaining lines. Add color.

A series of zigzag lines inside the propeller make it look like it's spinning. Add a few straight lines behind the plane to make it appear to be zipping through the air.

Silly Plane

Since there are no rules in cartooning, you can even bend a airplane's body to make it more expressive. Let's draw a silly plane.

1 Look at this silly shape. Lightly sketch curved lines to begin the head and body of the plane.

2 Add curved lines for wings and a tail.

3 Draw the curved windshield. Add the mouth. Draw two ovals for a propeller.

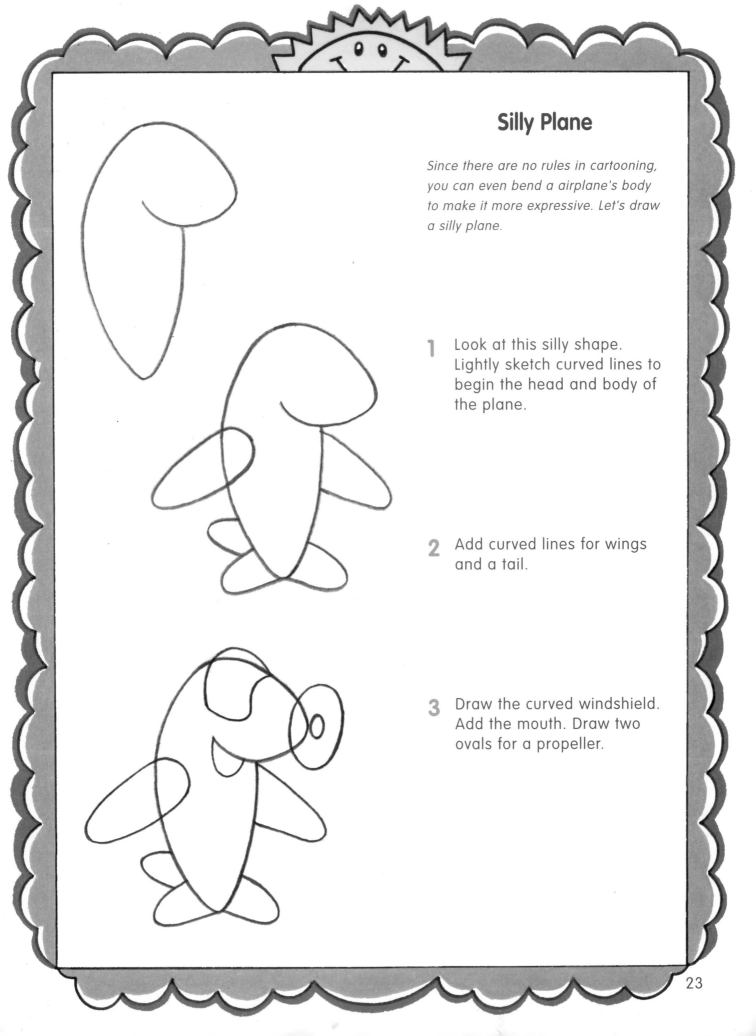

4 Add eyeballs. Draw a straight nose line next to the propeller. Add zigzag lines inside the propeller to make it look like it's spinning.

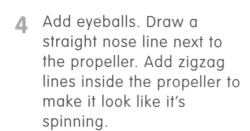

5 Draw a curved line along the side. Add windows. Draw curved lines inside the mouth for teeth and a tongue.

6 Look closely! Erase extra sketch lines. Darken the final lines. Add color.

Curved lines beneath the wings and body make the silly plane look like it's flying. If you draw a shadow under the tail, the silly plane will look like it's standing upright.

This silly plane sure looks happy for one that's bent out of shape!

Clothing

You can give your cartoon plane even more personality by adding clothing. Draw the silly plane again wearing a pilot's cap.

1 Sketch a kidney bean shape for the body. (Tip: It looks kind of like a squashed oval.)

2 Sketch curved lines for wings and a tail.

3 Draw slanted ovals for goggles. Add the eyes. Draw a squashed oval for the tail wing.

Draw the plane again wearing a silly hat you create.

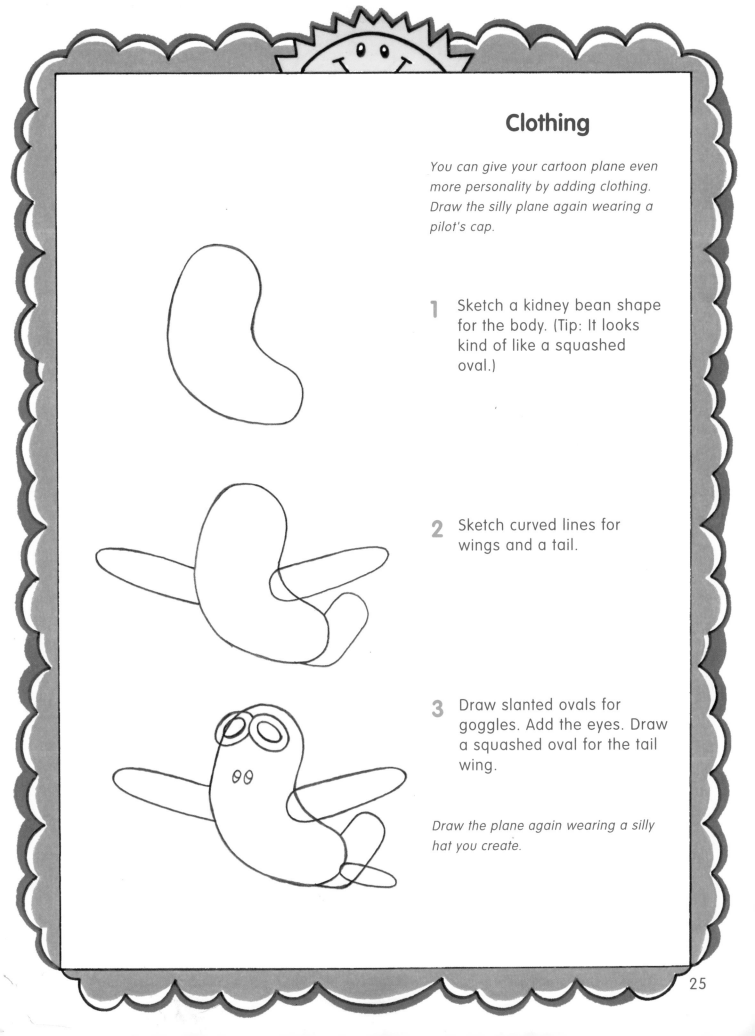

4 Draw the curved hat band. Add the flaps.

5 Look at the facial expression. Draw the lines and shapes you see.

6 Look closely! Erase extra lines. Darken the remaining lines. Add color.

It's "plane" to see that this pilot is in charge.

Pontoon Plane

Pontoon planes, also known as seaplanes, have floats instead of wheels. They can land on the surface of a lake, or on the ocean, and then drive to their docks like a boat. Let's draw a pontoon plane.

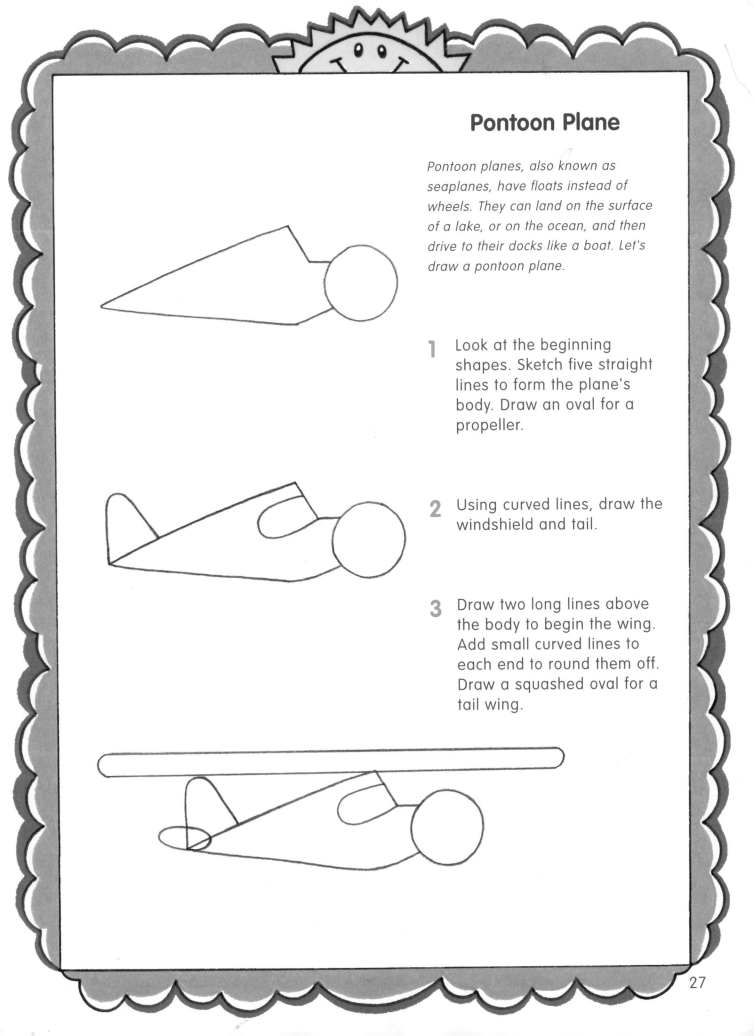

1 Look at the beginning shapes. Sketch five straight lines to form the plane's body. Draw an oval for a propeller.

2 Using curved lines, draw the windshield and tail.

3 Draw two long lines above the body to begin the wing. Add small curved lines to each end to round them off. Draw a squashed oval for a tail wing.

4 Look closely! What additional shapes and lines do you see? Starting at the top, add the support struts under the wings. Using curved lines, draw the pontoons. Using straight lines, draw the struts that connect the body and the pontoons.

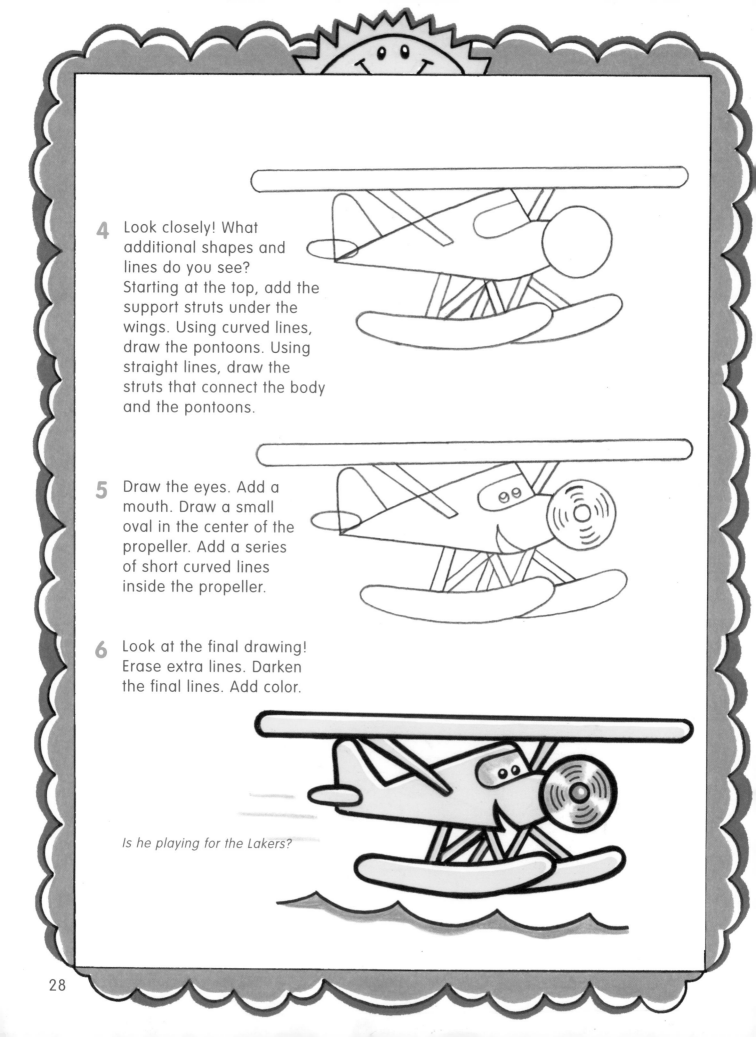

5 Draw the eyes. Add a mouth. Draw a small oval in the center of the propeller. Add a series of short curved lines inside the propeller.

6 Look at the final drawing! Erase extra lines. Darken the final lines. Add color.

Is he playing for the Lakers?

Biplane

Many early airplanes had two sets of wings. They were called biplanes and were used during World War I. Biplanes are also used in stunt shows and to dust crops in farmers' fields. Let's draw a biplane.

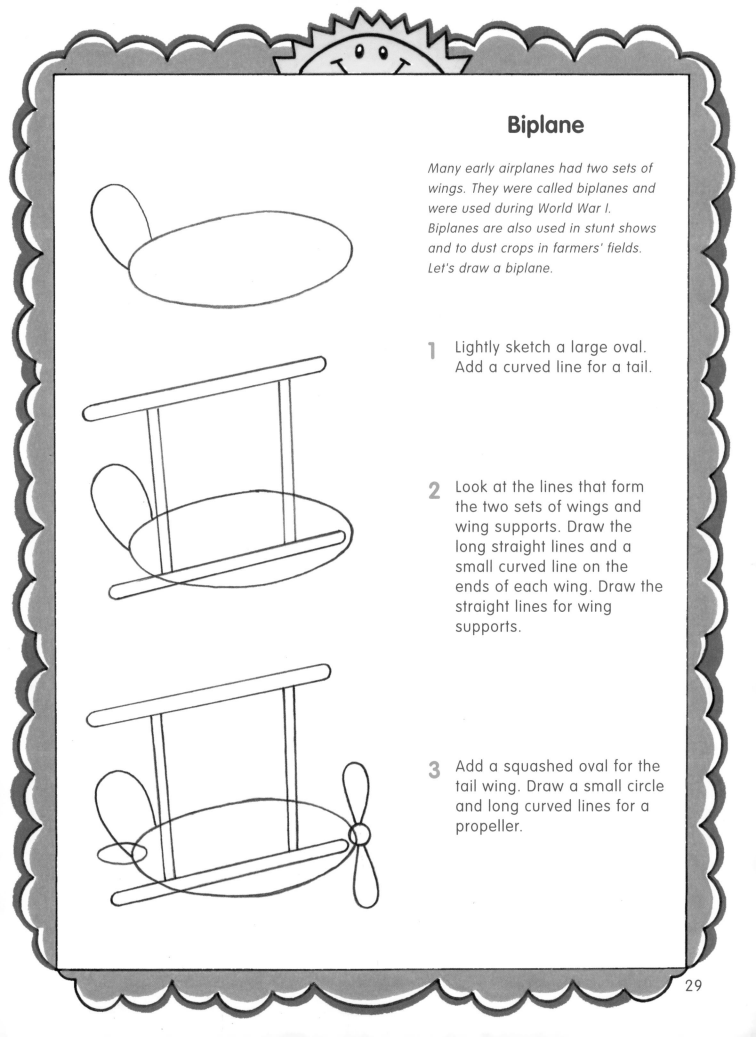

1 Lightly sketch a large oval. Add a curved line for a tail.

2 Look at the lines that form the two sets of wings and wing supports. Draw the long straight lines and a small curved line on the ends of each wing. Draw the straight lines for wing supports.

3 Add a squashed oval for the tail wing. Draw a small circle and long curved lines for a propeller.

4 Draw a curved line for the cockpit. Add straight lines under the body for wheel struts and a small oval for the center of the wheel.

5 Draw a straight line on the side of the body. Look at the wheel. Add straight lines for wheel spokes. Draw two ovals for the tire.

6 Look closely! Erase extra sketch lines. Darken the final lines. Add color.

Who is that goofy pilot? Check out the next two pages to find out how to add a pilot to your biplane.

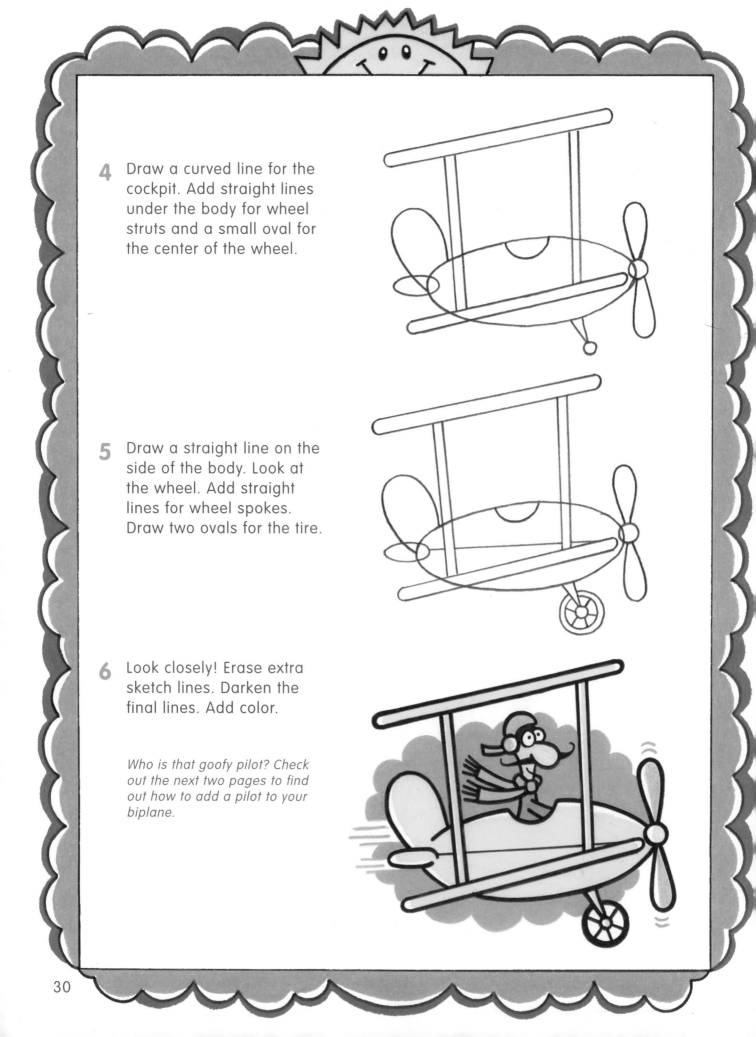

Add a Goofy Pilot

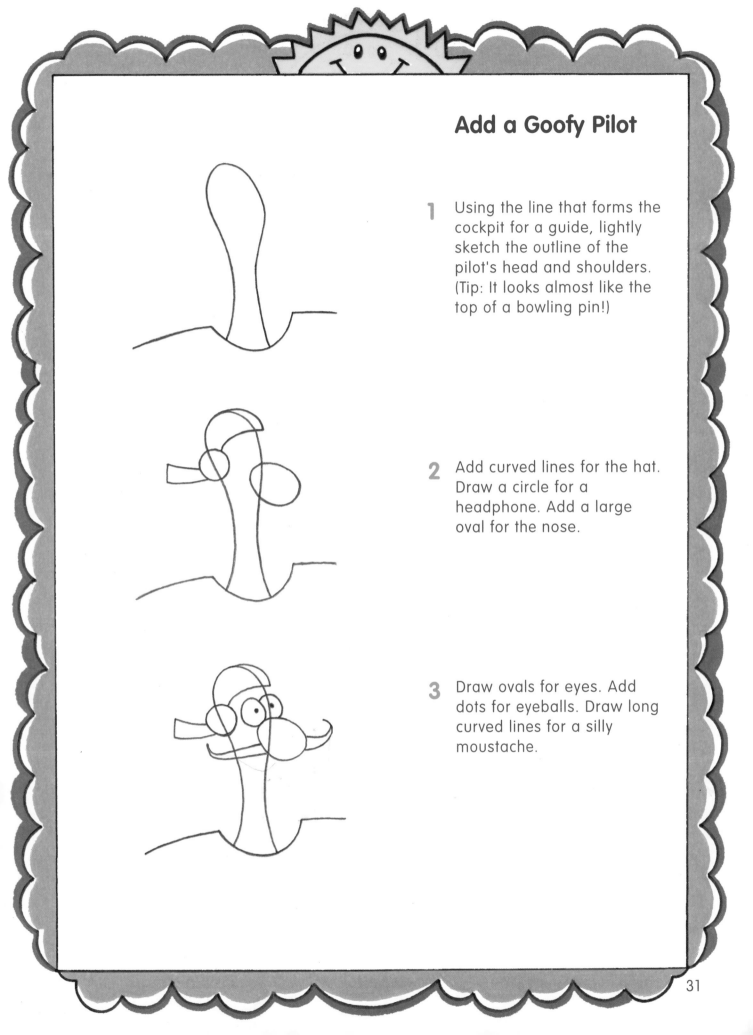

1 Using the line that forms the cockpit for a guide, lightly sketch the outline of the pilot's head and shoulders. (Tip: It looks almost like the top of a bowling pin!)

2 Add curved lines for the hat. Draw a circle for a headphone. Add a large oval for the nose.

3 Draw ovals for eyes. Add dots for eyeballs. Draw long curved lines for a silly moustache.

4 Add a curved line for a smile. Draw curved lines to begin his flowing scarf.

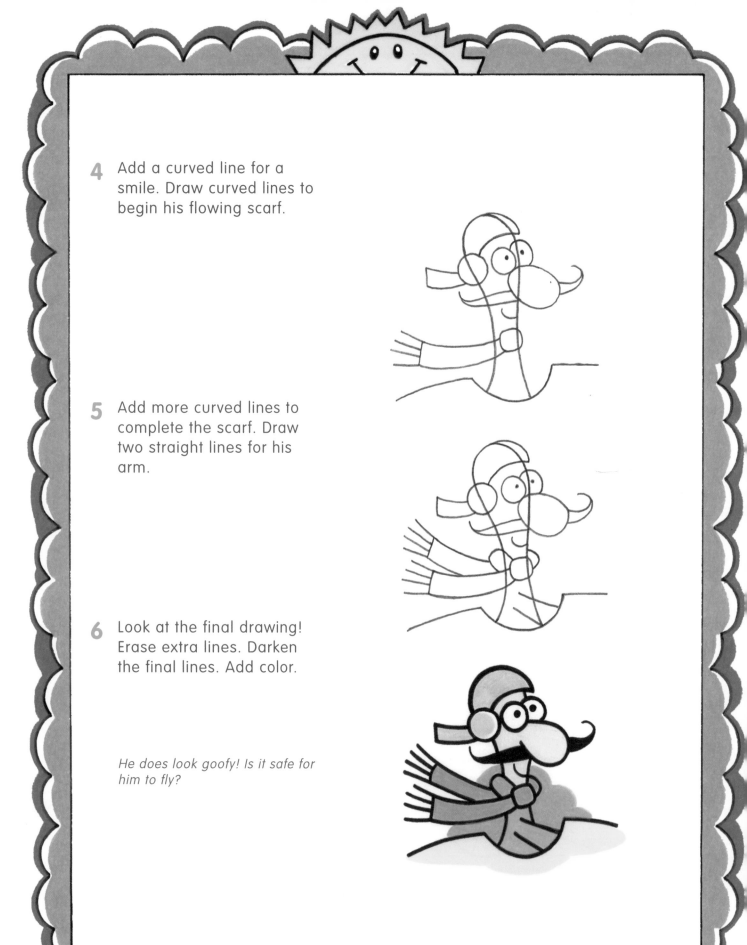

5 Add more curved lines to complete the scarf. Draw two straight lines for his arm.

6 Look at the final drawing! Erase extra lines. Darken the final lines. Add color.

He does look goofy! Is it safe for him to fly?

Simple Helicopter

Cartoon drawing can be very simple. Let's draw a simple helicopter, then draw a more detailed one in the next lesson.

1 Lightly sketch an egg shape for the helicopter's body.

2 Draw a large oval with a smaller oval in the center for a propeller. Add two straight lines to connect it to the body.

3 Add the curved windshield. Look at the tail and rear propeller. Draw curved lines for a tail and two small circles for the rear propeller.

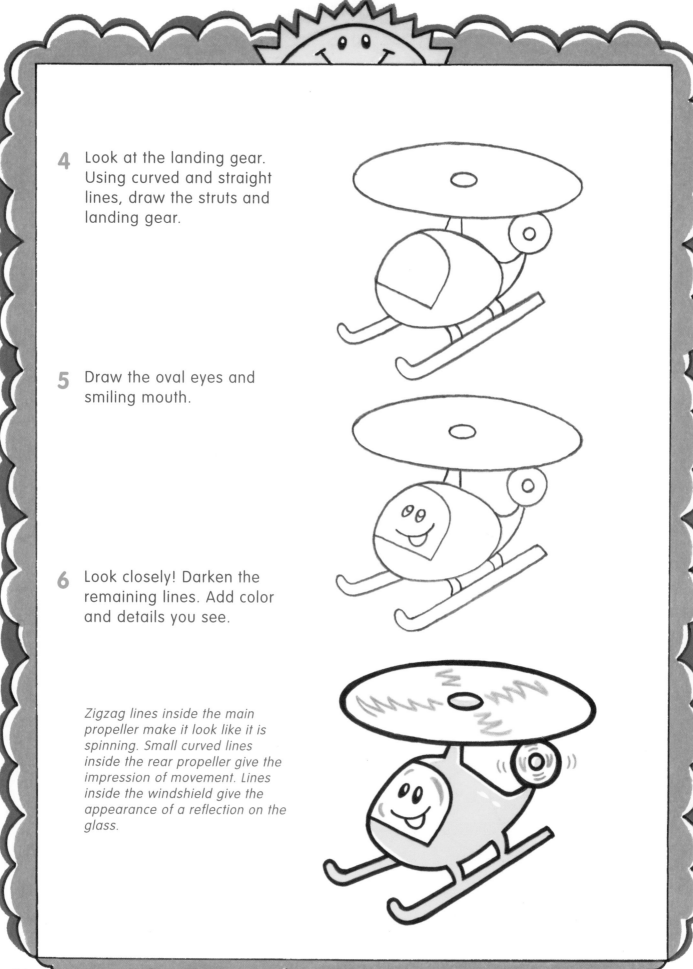

4 Look at the landing gear. Using curved and straight lines, draw the struts and landing gear.

5 Draw the oval eyes and smiling mouth.

6 Look closely! Darken the remaining lines. Add color and details you see.

Zigzag lines inside the main propeller make it look like it is spinning. Small curved lines inside the rear propeller give the impression of movement. Lines inside the windshield give the appearance of a reflection on the glass.

News Helicopter

This helicopter will be a little more detailed than the one we just drew. Look closely! Follow directions and you'll end up with a great cartoon helicopter.

1 Lightly sketch a half-oval shape for the body. Draw two long curved lines for the tail.

2 Look at the shapes forming the gears of the main propeller. Draw the shapes you see. Look at the rear propeller. Draw the ovals and square shape you see.

3 Draw the main propeller. Add a small curved line above it. Draw curved lines for the windshield and door.

4 Draw curved lines inside the rear propeller. Look at the landing gear. Draw it.

5 Draw the oval eyes and big smile. Add curved lines outside the rear rotor to show movement and a curved dotted line behind the helicopter to show it lifting off.

6 Look at the final drawing! Go over and darken the final lines. Add color.

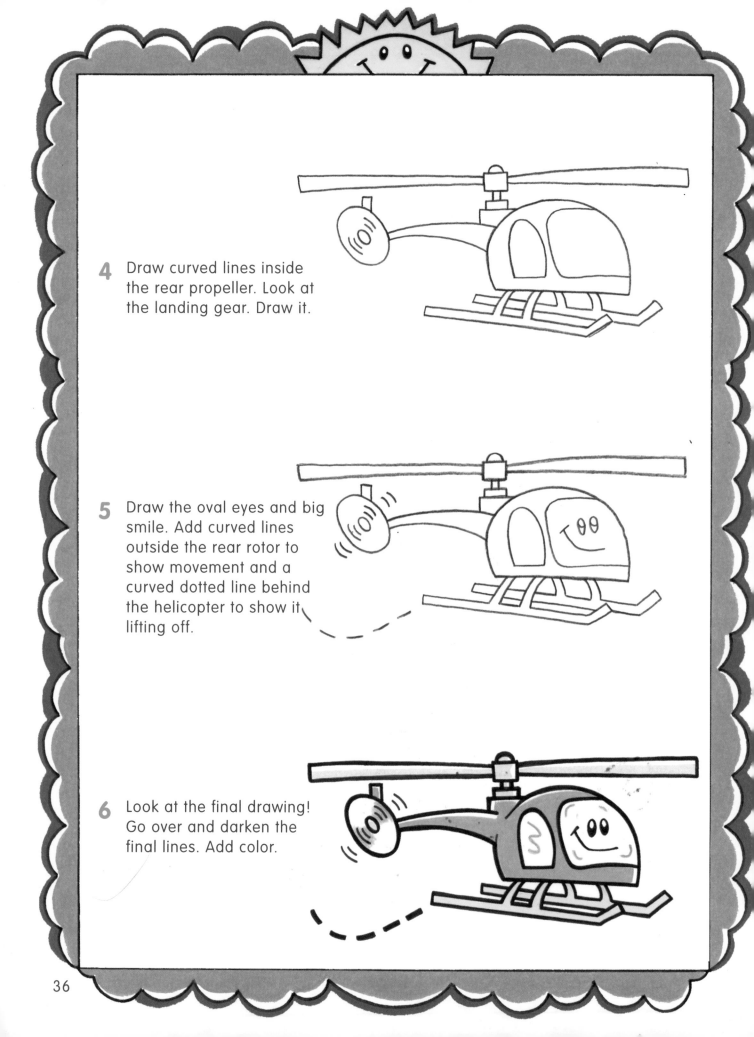

Private Jet

Many of the world's wealthiest people own their own private jets. They hire a personal pilot to fly them anywhere they want to go. Let's draw a streamlined personal jet.

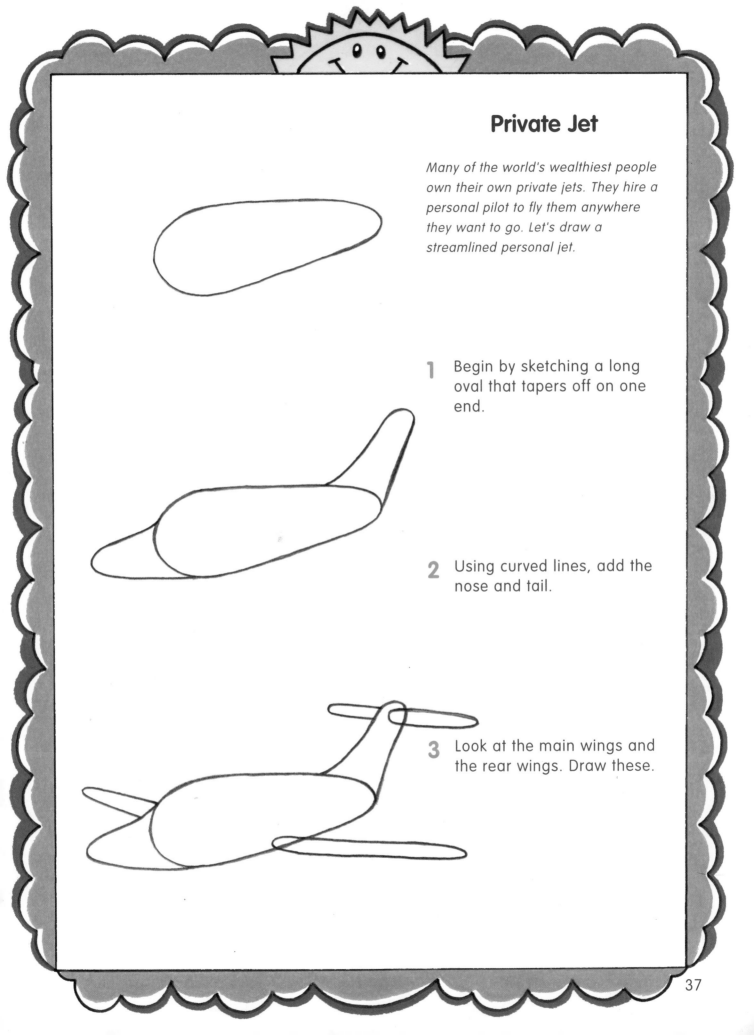

1 Begin by sketching a long oval that tapers off on one end.

2 Using curved lines, add the nose and tail.

3 Look at the main wings and the rear wings. Draw these.

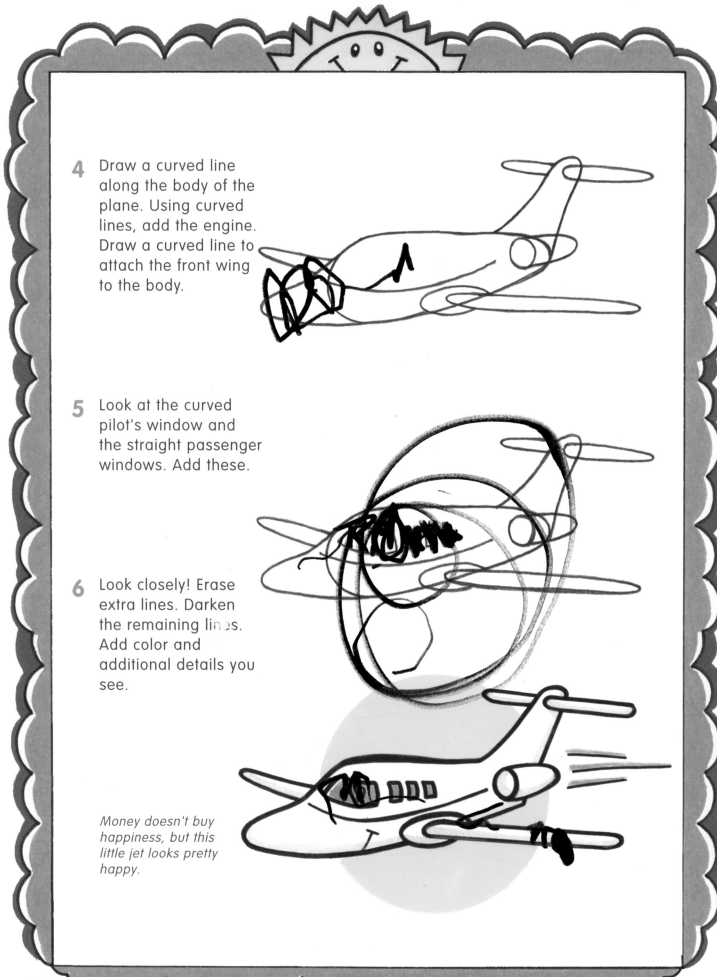

4 Draw a curved line along the body of the plane. Using curved lines, add the engine. Draw a curved line to attach the front wing to the body.

5 Look at the curved pilot's window and the straight passenger windows. Add these.

6 Look closely! Erase extra lines. Darken the remaining lines. Add color and additional details you see.

Money doesn't buy happiness, but this little jet looks pretty happy.

Fighter Jet

The military uses a variety of fighter jets to patrol the skies during times of peace and to attack during times of war. Wouldn't it be nice if we didn't need them anymore? Let's draw a cartoon fighter jet.

1 Look closely at this shape. Using curved lines, sketch it lightly.

2 Starting at the top, draw curved lines for a cockpit. Look closely at the shape of the tail, engine, and wings. Add these.

3 Look again! Add missiles to the wings. Draw the jet engine on top, near the tail.

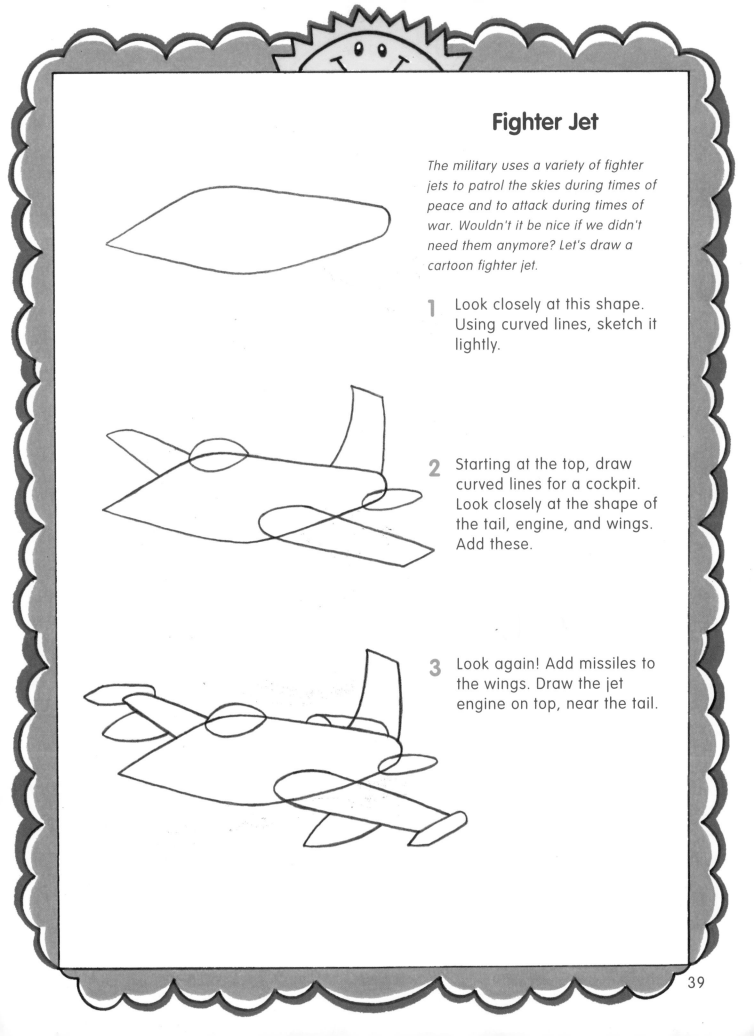

4 Draw curved lines for an eye and eyebrow. Add sharp, curved lines for a mouth. Add a curved line on each missile.

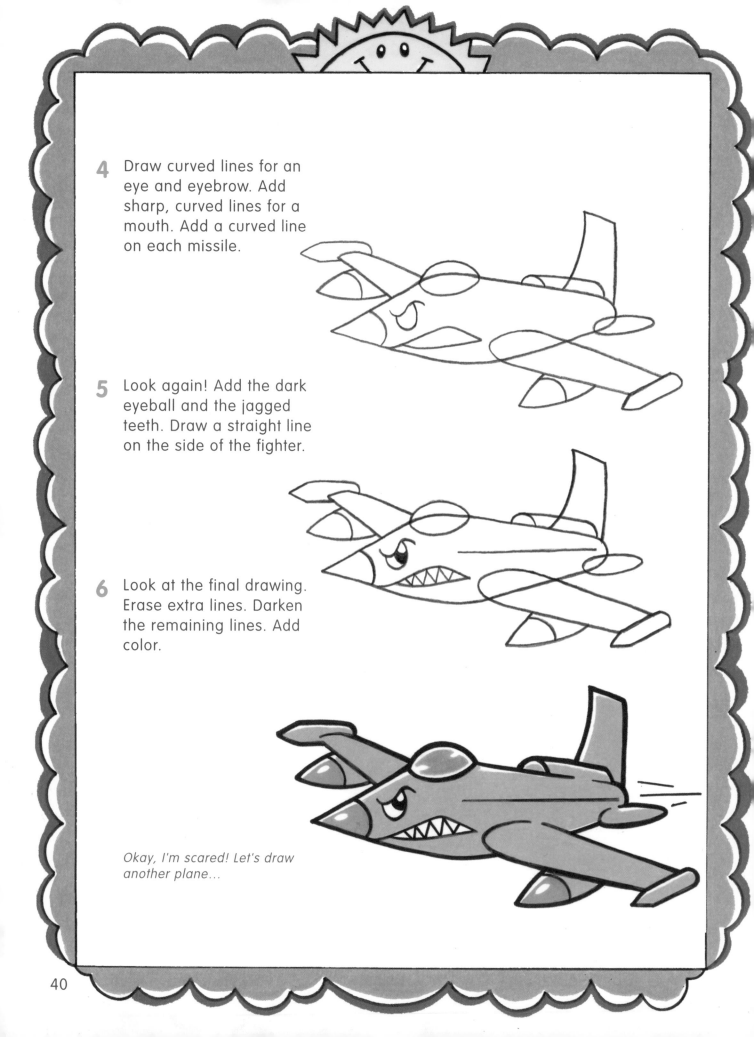

5 Look again! Add the dark eyeball and the jagged teeth. Draw a straight line on the side of the fighter.

6 Look at the final drawing. Erase extra lines. Darken the remaining lines. Add color.

Okay, I'm scared! Let's draw another plane…

Commercial Airliner

We drew a passenger jet earlier in this book. Let's draw a more realistic commercial airliner.

1 Look closely at the shape of the body. Using curved lines, sketch the long shape. If you don't get it right the first time, use your eraser and fix it until you are happy with the results.

2 Look at the shapes of the wings and tail. Draw these.

3 Starting at the front, add the nose cone and windshield. Draw the tail wings.

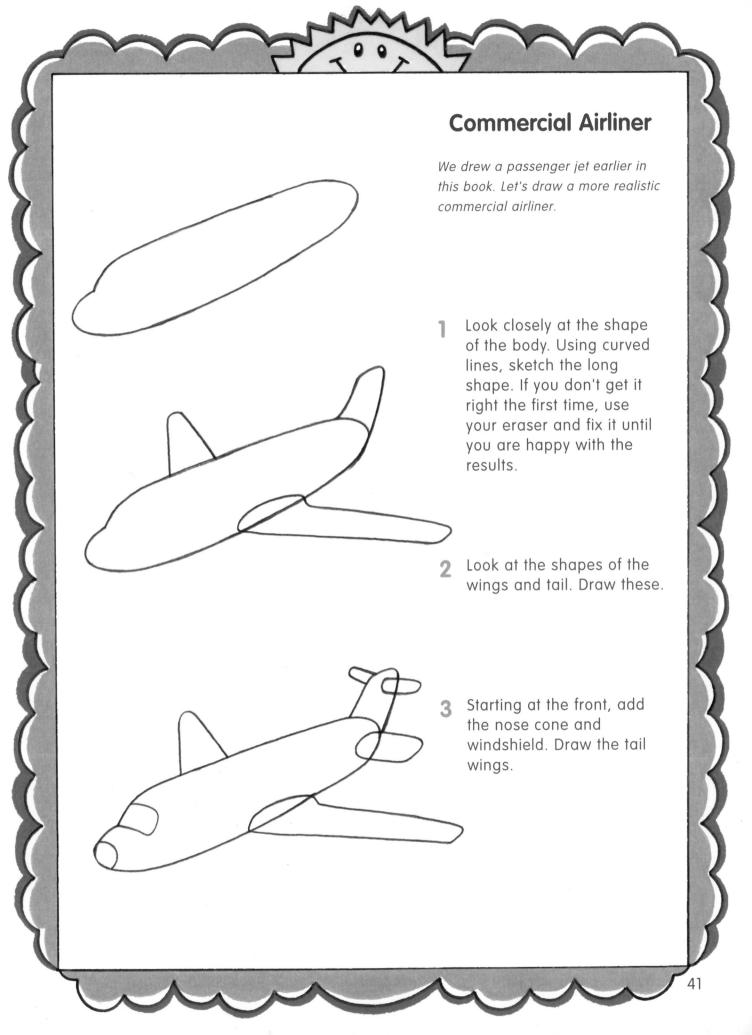

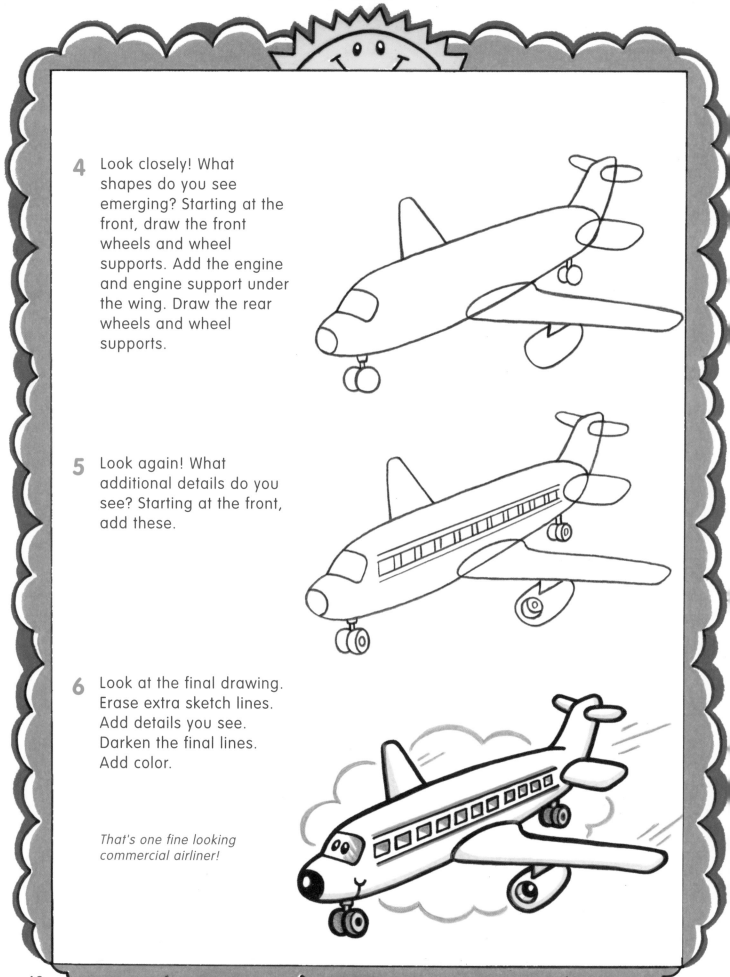

4 Look closely! What shapes do you see emerging? Starting at the front, draw the front wheels and wheel supports. Add the engine and engine support under the wing. Draw the rear wheels and wheel supports.

5 Look again! What additional details do you see? Starting at the front, add these.

6 Look at the final drawing. Erase extra sketch lines. Add details you see. Darken the final lines. Add color.

That's one fine looking commercial airliner!

Jumbo Jet

Jumbo jets are gigantic aircraft. They carry many more passengers than most other commercial airliners. They usually have two floors of passenger seats inside instead of one. Let's draw a jumbo jet.

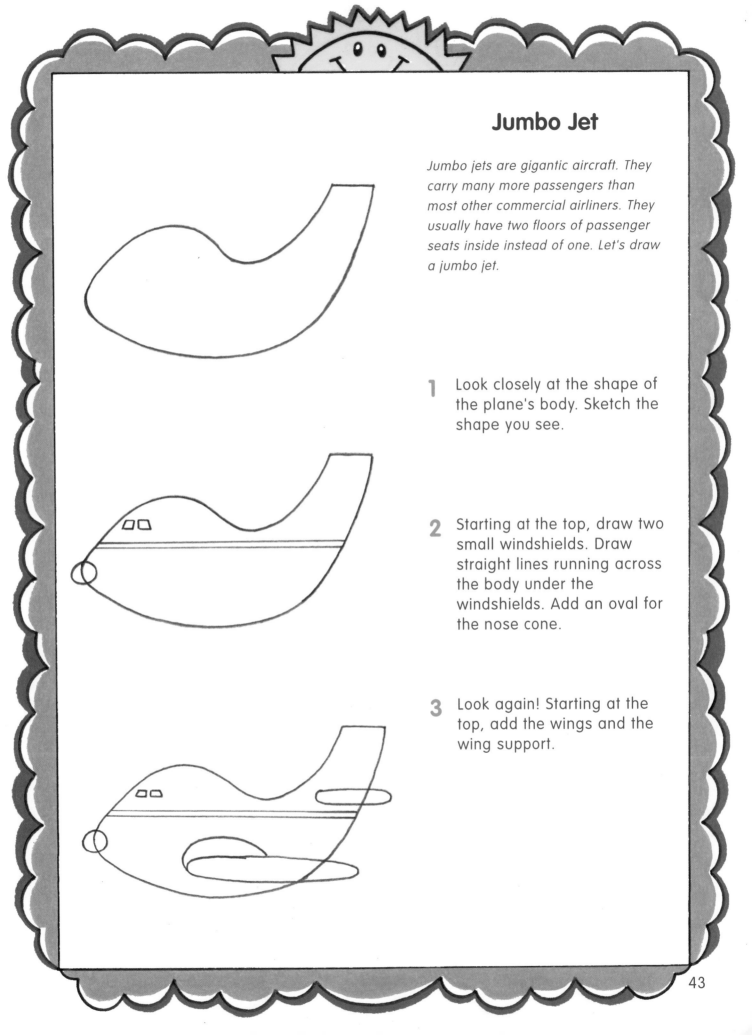

1 Look closely at the shape of the plane's body. Sketch the shape you see.

2 Starting at the top, draw two small windshields. Draw straight lines running across the body under the windshields. Add an oval for the nose cone.

3 Look again! Starting at the top, add the wings and the wing support.

4 Draw two curved lines for a happy mouth. Draw straight lines under the body for landing gear.

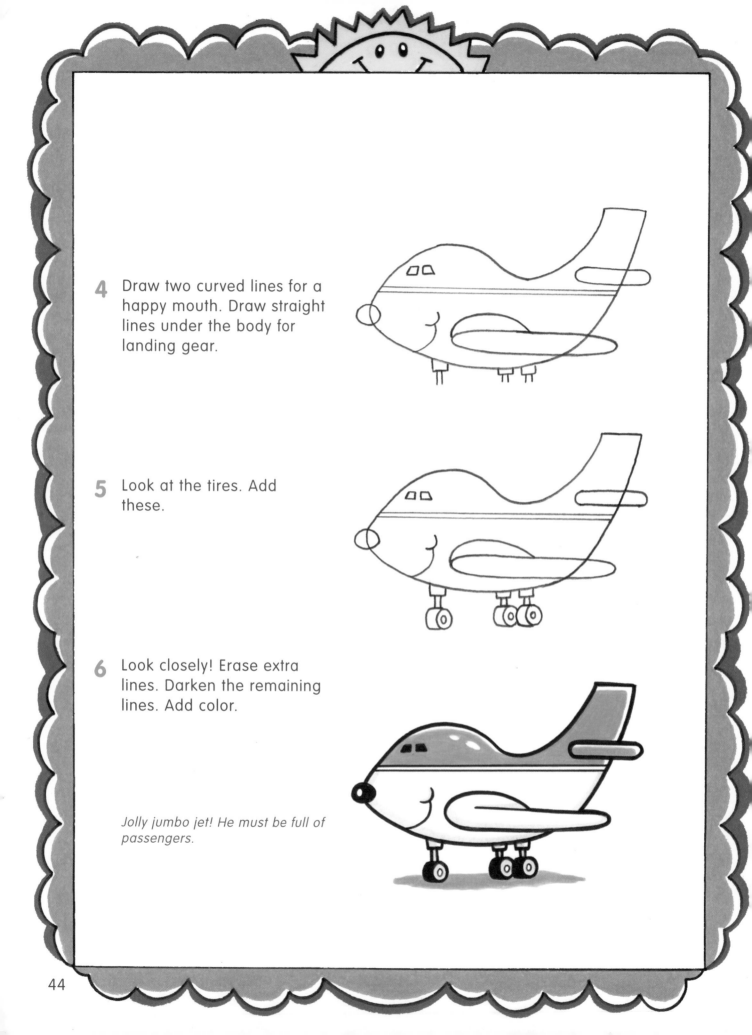

5 Look at the tires. Add these.

6 Look closely! Erase extra lines. Darken the remaining lines. Add color.

Jolly jumbo jet! He must be full of passengers.

Space Shuttle

The space shuttle is an incredible aircraft! It can fly in outer space, then return to the earth's atmosphere and land like a jet. Let's draw a space shuttle.

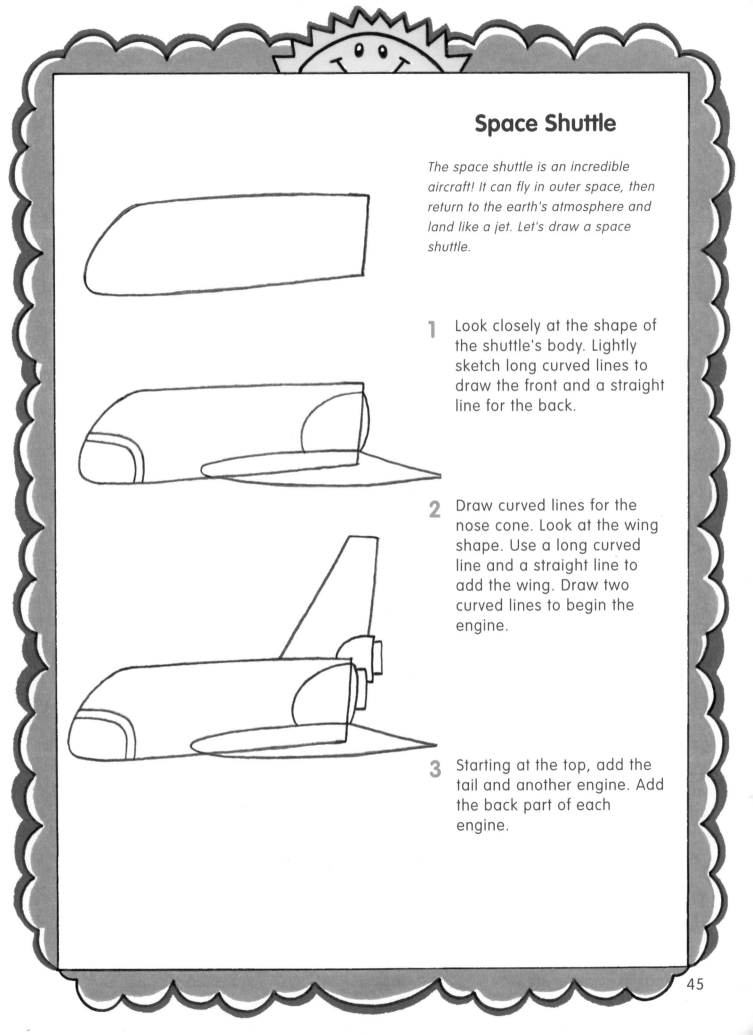

1 Look closely at the shape of the shuttle's body. Lightly sketch long curved lines to draw the front and a straight line for the back.

2 Draw curved lines for the nose cone. Look at the wing shape. Use a long curved line and a straight line to add the wing. Draw two curved lines to begin the engine.

3 Starting at the top, add the tail and another engine. Add the back part of each engine.

4 Look at the details emerging. Starting at the front, add the details you see.

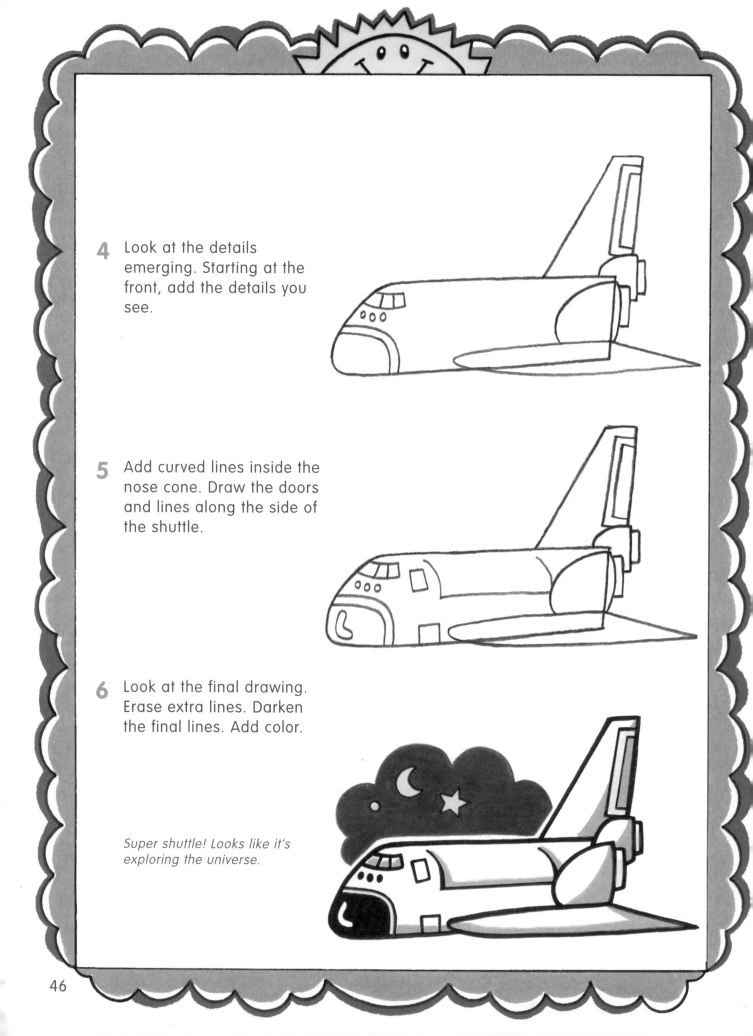

5 Add curved lines inside the nose cone. Draw the doors and lines along the side of the shuttle.

6 Look at the final drawing. Erase extra lines. Darken the final lines. Add color.

Super shuttle! Looks like it's exploring the universe.

Landing

Let's draw a commercial airliner coming in for a landing on a runway.

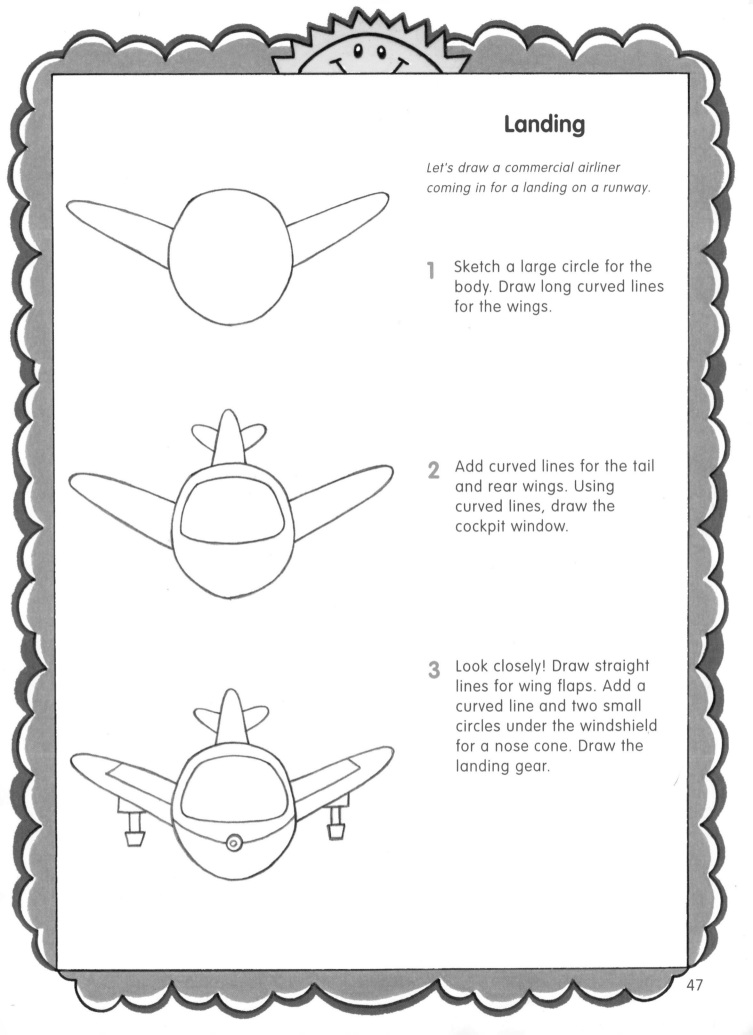

1 Sketch a large circle for the body. Draw long curved lines for the wings.

2 Add curved lines for the tail and rear wings. Using curved lines, draw the cockpit window.

3 Look closely! Draw straight lines for wing flaps. Add a curved line and two small circles under the windshield for a nose cone. Draw the landing gear.

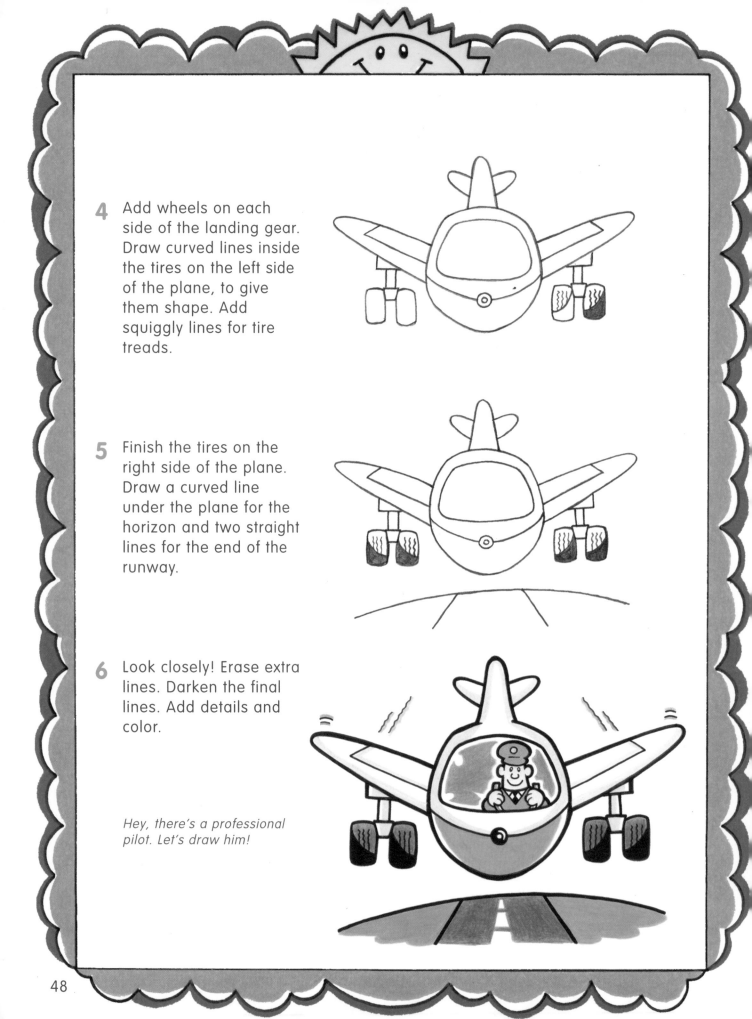

4 Add wheels on each side of the landing gear. Draw curved lines inside the tires on the left side of the plane, to give them shape. Add squiggly lines for tire treads.

5 Finish the tires on the right side of the plane. Draw a curved line under the plane for the horizon and two straight lines for the end of the runway.

6 Look closely! Erase extra lines. Darken the final lines. Add details and color.

Hey, there's a professional pilot. Let's draw him!

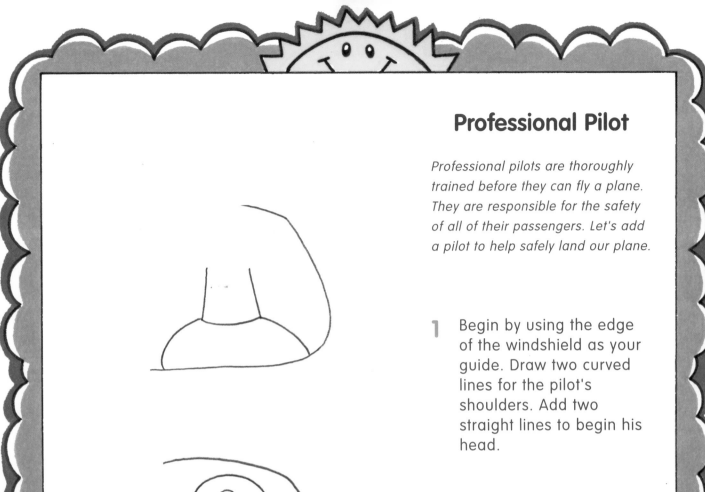

Professional Pilot

Professional pilots are thoroughly trained before they can fly a plane. They are responsible for the safety of all of their passengers. Let's add a pilot to help safely land our plane.

1 Begin by using the edge of the windshield as your guide. Draw two curved lines for the pilot's shoulders. Add two straight lines to begin his head.

2 Add curved lines on each side of his head for ears. Look at the shape of his hat. Draw the squashed ovals for his hat and brim. Add a small circle inside the top of the hat.

3 Look again! Draw his eyes, nose, and mouth. Using curved lines, draw his two hands.

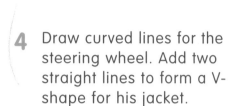

4 Draw curved lines for the steering wheel. Add two straight lines to form a V-shape for his jacket.

5 Look at his shirt collar and tie. Add these.

6 Look at the final drawing. Darken part of the eyes and the final lines. Add color.

Great job!

Sketch, doodle, and play! Add eyelashes and long hair to turn your pilot into a woman! Change the shape of the head. See what you can come up with to make the pilot look really different.

Stealth Plane

Stealth planes can fly at incredible speeds and altitudes without being detected by radar. They are made of special materials that are difficult for radar and other equipment to see. They look almost like craft from another planet. Let's draw a stealth plane.

1 Lightly sketch a large triangle.

2 Look closely! That's the crew compartment emerging.

3 Draw straight lines in a zigzag pattern to shape the wings.

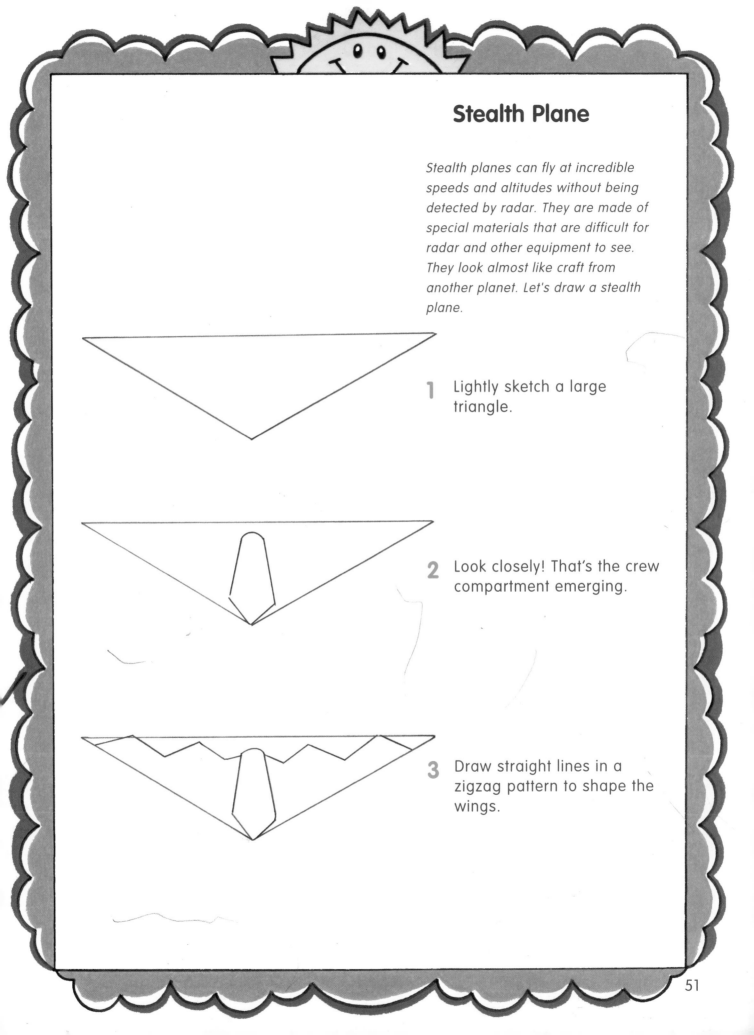

4 Look at the engines. Draw an engine on each side of the crew compartment.

5 Look at that face! Add the windows, eyes and eyebrows. Add straight lines inside the wings.

6 Look closely! Erase extra sketch lines. Darken the remaining lines. Add color.

Excellent job! That's one sneaky looking stealth plane.

Airport

Our planes need somewhere to land and takeoff. Let's draw an airport for them to call home.

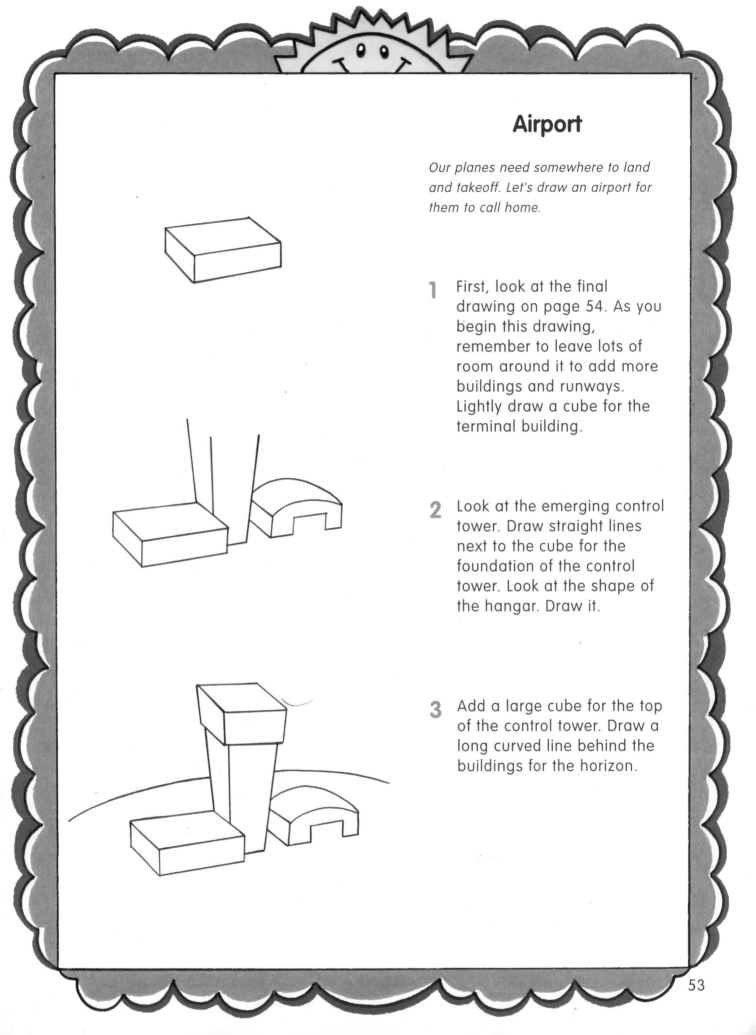

1 First, look at the final drawing on page 54. As you begin this drawing, remember to leave lots of room around it to add more buildings and runways. Lightly draw a cube for the terminal building.

2 Look at the emerging control tower. Draw straight lines next to the cube for the foundation of the control tower. Look at the shape of the hangar. Draw it.

3 Add a large cube for the top of the control tower. Draw a long curved line behind the buildings for the horizon.

4 Look at the details added to this drawing. Starting at the top, add the control tower windows. Draw the terminal windows and door. Using straight lines, add the runways.

5 Look at the final drawing. Darken the final lines. Add color. Draw a few of your favorite cartoon aircraft circling above the airport.

Plane from Above

Another fun way to draw scenery for a cartoon airplane is to look straight down at the plane. Let's draw a plane from above, then add the ground below.

1 Draw a long, squashed oval for the plane's body.

2 Look at the shape of the wings. Draw a wing on each side. Add a small oval for the tail.

3 Starting at the top, draw a curved line for the nose cone. Use curved lines to begin the engines on the wings. Look at the tail and back wings. Add these.

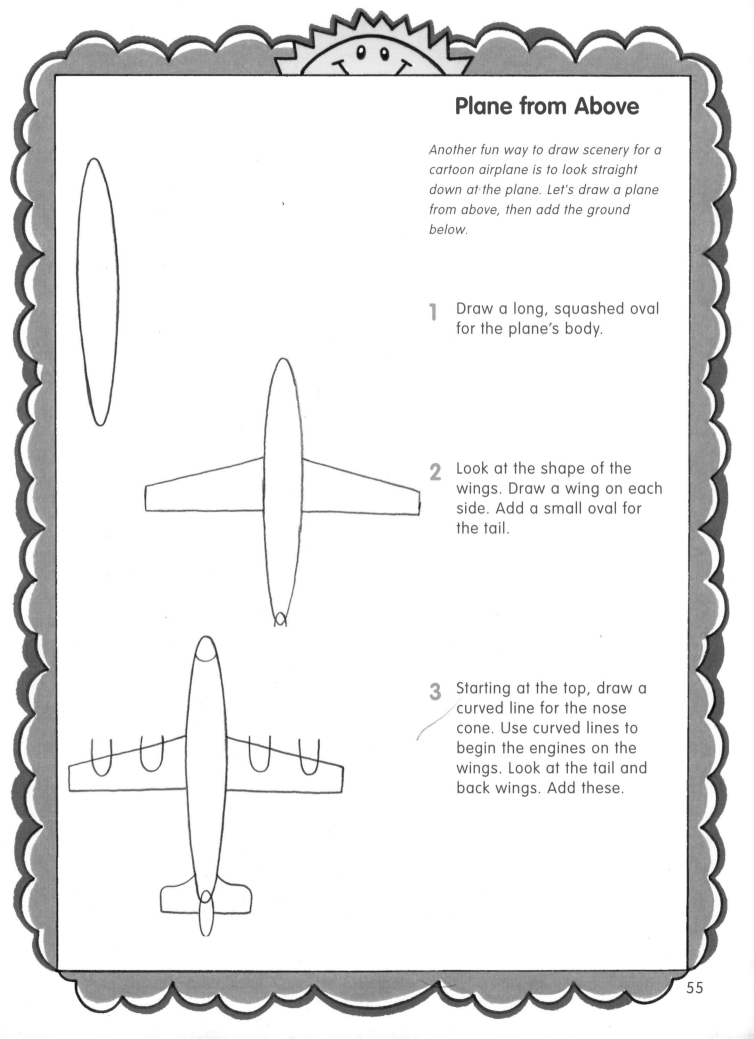

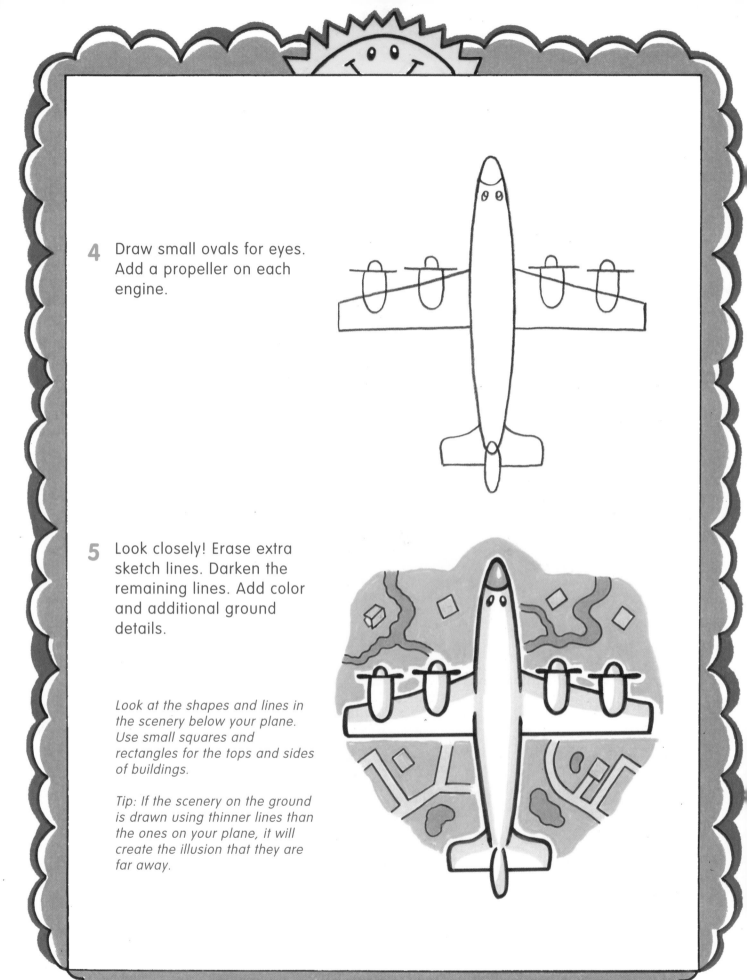

4   Draw small ovals for eyes. Add a propeller on each engine.

5   Look closely! Erase extra sketch lines. Darken the remaining lines. Add color and additional ground details.

Look at the shapes and lines in the scenery below your plane. Use small squares and rectangles for the tops and sides of buildings.

Tip: If the scenery on the ground is drawn using thinner lines than the ones on your plane, it will create the illusion that they are far away.

Hang glider

Some daring people like to fly without a plane! They are hang gliders and they fly using something that looks like a large kite. They launch their craft from mountain top or large sand dunes near the ocean. Let's draw a hang glider.

1 Look closely at the beginning shapes. Sketch these.

2 Add the eyes and nose. Draw curved lines for arms. Add a curved line for the bottom of his shirt and a straight line for legs. Draw the feet.

3 Starting at the top, add eyebrows, a hair line, an ear, and a big smile. Draw circles for hands.

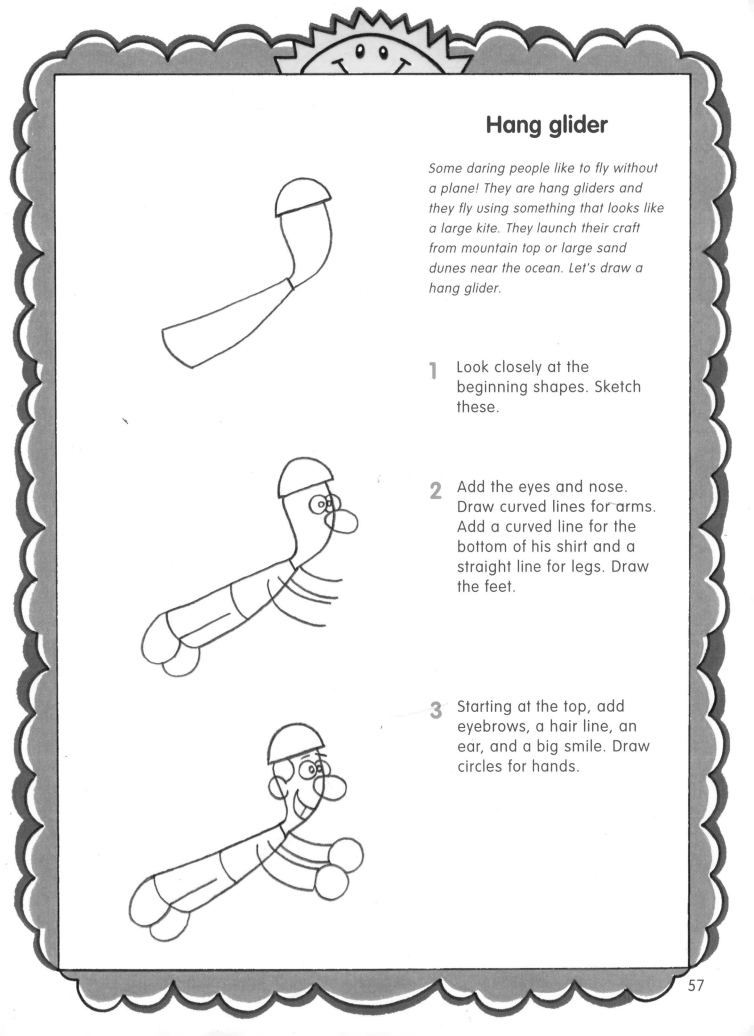

4 Draw a long curved line above him to begin the hang glider. Add lines to his helmet and hair. Draw lines for the glider's grip. Add finger lines

5 Look at the shape of the glider. Add the lines you see.

6 Look at the final drawing. Erase extra sketch lines. Darken the remaining lines. Add color.

Use different facial and hair lines to change your hang glider into a girl. You may want to make her nose a little smaller too!

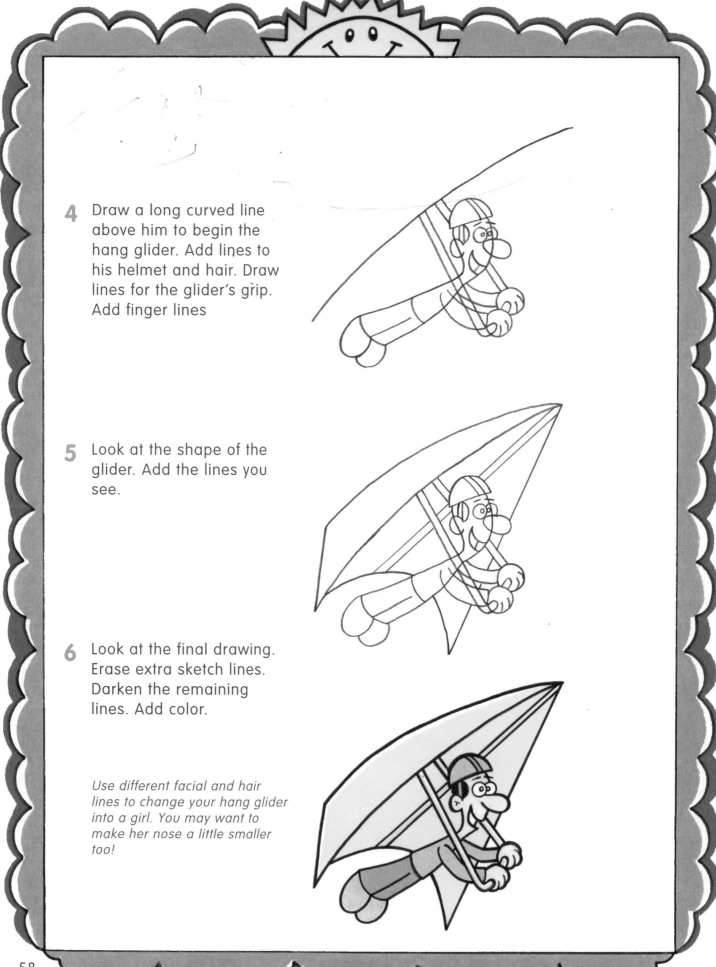

Jet Pack

Still other adventuresome souls try to fly with personal jet packs. Maybe some day we will all travel that way instead of using cars. I sure hope people can fly better than they can drive!

1 Sketch an oval for the helmet. Draw curved lines to begin the body.

2 Look at the details inside the helmet shape. Starting at the top, draw the face and helmet lines. Add a straight line for the legs. Draw the shoes.

3 Add the eyebrow, eye, and nose. Draw the arm and hand. Using curved lines, begin the jet pack.

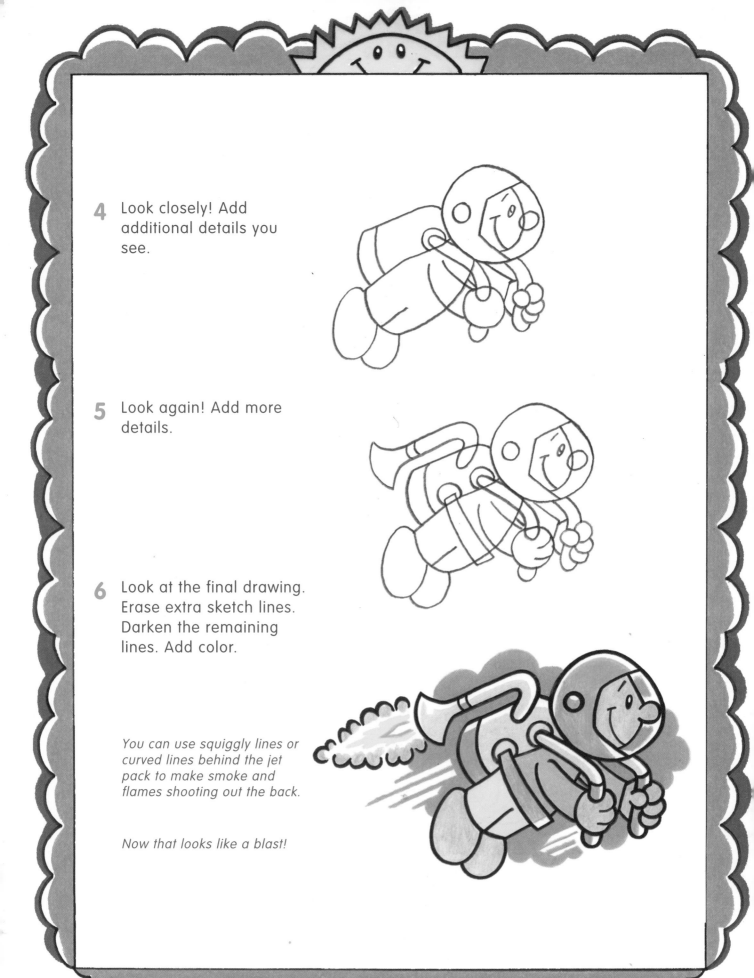

4 Look closely! Add additional details you see.

5 Look again! Add more details.

6 Look at the final drawing. Erase extra sketch lines. Darken the remaining lines. Add color.

You can use squiggly lines or curved lines behind the jet pack to make smoke and flames shooting out the back.

Now that looks like a blast!

Keep Going!

Don't stop now! This is just the beginning of becoming a talented cartoon artist. Keep practicing and experimenting.

Try doodling aimlessly with your pencil held loosely in your hand. Let shapes come out of the end of your pencil, then see what kind of cartoon you can create with them! See if you can draw airplanes from different angles.

Ready? Set? GO!

Experiment!

Experiment with different shapes and lines. Try combining different features from the aircraft you've drawn to create a new flying machine no one else has ever seen.

Try putting wings and tails on cars, trucks, or whatever else you can imagine. Drawing cartoons is a wild, wacky way to have lots of fun.

Now that you know how to use simple lines and shapes to create cool cartoon characters, keep practicing. You will be amazed at how talented you really are!

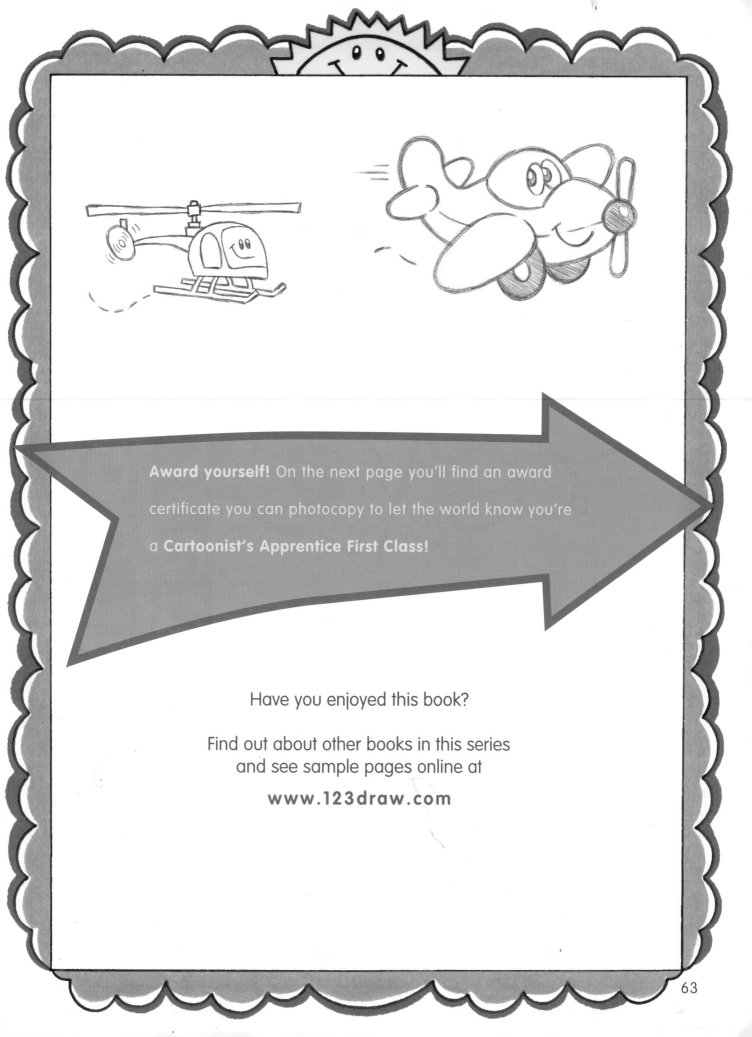

Award yourself! On the next page you'll find an award certificate you can photocopy to let the world know you're a **Cartoonist's Apprentice First Class!**

Have you enjoyed this book?

Find out about other books in this series
and see sample pages online at

www.123draw.com

Cartoonist's Apprentice

THIS IS TO CERTIFY THAT

(APPRENTICE'S NAME)

HAS SUCCESSFULLY
COMPLETED THE
"1-2-3 DRAW CARTOON
AIRCRAFT" DRAWING
COURSE.

_____
DATE

Steve Barr
INSTRUCTOR